MAKING YOUR OWN
CROSS STITCH GIFTS

SHEILA COULSON

NEW HOLLAND

First published in 1994 by
New Holland (Publishers) Ltd
London • Cape Town • Sydney • Singapore

24 Nutford Place
London W1H 6DQ
United Kingdom

80 McKenzie Street
Cape Town 8001
South Africa

3/2 Aquatic Drive
Frenchs Forest, NSW 2086
Australia

Reprinted in 1997

I would like to thank DMC, and in particular,
Cara Ackerman and Maria Diaz at DMC Creative
World, for supplying me with all the embroidery
fabrics and threads used in this book.

Also thanks to Liz Elvin at the Royal School of
Needlework at Hampton Court Palace, England,
for allowing me to use one of the school's original
Berlin Woolwork charts for the curtain tie-back
design on page 50.

ISBN 1 85368 220 9 (hb)
ISBN 1 85368 326 4 (pb)

Creative Editor: Pauline Butler
Assistant Editor: Sue Thraves
Art Director: Jane Forster
Photographer: ShonaWood
Illustrator: Terry Evans
Calligrapher: David Harris

Phototypeset by Ace Filmsetting Ltd, Frome,
Somerset
Reproduction by Scantrans Pte Ltd, Singapore
Printed and bound in Singapore by Kyodo
Printing Co (Pte) Ltd

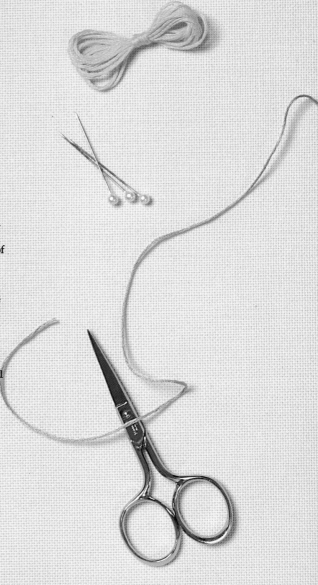

Contents

Introduction

Cross stitch has long been a popular form of embroidery in many countries around the world. The embroidered household linens and peasant costumes of Greece, Russia, Scandinavia, India, North Africa and Eastern Europe all provide a rich and delightful source of traditional patterns and designs.

In Europe, the working of cross stitch samplers became common in the last century as a schoolroom activity to teach young girls the art of the needle. These samplers, like the peasant embroideries of other parts of the world, provide an insight into the lifestyles of these people and offer lots of decorative possibilities for modern cross stitch projects. In this book of gift ideas I have tried to incorporate some of these traditional forms of cross stitch in a way that makes them accessible to even an inexperienced embroiderer.

One of the delights of cross stitch lies in the fact that it is such an easy technique to learn, so that with a little basic knowledge, even a beginner can achieve attractive results. For many people cross stitch is, in fact, the first embroidery stitch they learn as children. I grew up with my mother's needlework activities all around me and at the age of about six or seven she put a needle in my hand and began to introduce me to some elementary embroidery stitches, among them cross stitch. A year or so ago I found history repeating itself as I started to teach my own daughter in the same way.

Enjoyment is an essential ingredient in the process of making a gift for someone – a good deal of the fun comes in the planning and selecting of the gift and anticipating the pleasure it will give.

However, enjoyment can be marred if you struggle with a project which is just beyond your capabilities, so I have tried in this book to present a range of gift ideas to suit all levels of skill. Some projects, such as the potholders in the **Gifts for the kitchen** chapter, or the needlecase and pincushion in the **Small gifts** chapter, could be tackled by a beginner as the designs are simple and use few colours. Other projects require a little more experience, though only the same basic skills are required for all the gifts. If you are new to cross stitch, you will soon gain confidence and be able to move on to the more testing projects.

As well as the level of your experience, the other important consideration when choosing which gift to make, is the amount of time available to you. There is nothing more calculated to kill your enjoyment than having to stitch too large an item in a rush.

Some projects such as the curtain tie-back or the bed linen in the **Gifts for the home** chapter require hours of work. Equally, there are projects that can be worked in one or two evenings. Most of those in the **Small gifts** chapter are in this category.

Having chosen your project, the main thing is to enjoy the process of making it. Embroidery should mean relaxation and pleasure – if not it is simply a tedious chore. I think it is worth remembering, that while you will want your work to be of as high a standard as possible, you are making a gift for someone, not entering a competition. So don't be over anxious to achieve absolute perfection, follow the basic rules for neat stitching and remember that in the majority of cases the back of the embroidery will be hidden and will not disgrace you!

With each project you will find full instructions for embroidering and making up the item. If any special sewing techniques are required, these are covered in the **Getting started** chapter.

Once you are familiar with some of the designs in the book, have a bit of fun with them – be creative and don't be afraid to experiment. Try different fabrics and colours of thread to change the feel of a design. Use a chart for a different purpose – the bed linen design on page 44, for example, could be applied to table linen; the ivy-leaf shelf edging could be used on a tray cloth; the primroses on page 67 could be stitched on larger count fabric with thicker thread and used to decorate the corner of a cushion. It is also worth noting that cross stitch charts can be used for canvaswork – one coloured square on the chart equals one stitch in just the same way.

Alternative materials
At the time of going to press, please note that the author has made every effort to ensure that the fabrics and threads used throughout this book are readily available. If, however, some materials are difficult to obtain, the following alternatives may be used: In place of Medici wool, other crewel embroidery wools are available in a wide range of colours.

Also flower thread, which is used in two projects, may be replaced by a single strand of stranded cotton. Flower thread colours can be converted to stranded cottons. Below are listed the stranded cotton equivalents to the flower threads used in the projects (stranded cotton numbers in brackets).

Primrose Card (page 67)
2742 (742), 2745 (745), 2727 (727), 2840 (840), 2906 (906), 2788 (704), 2909 (910)
Trinket Box (page 86)
2743 (744), 2394 (550), 2210 (210), 2359 (340), 2369 (368), 2502 (502)

In addition, please note that Oslo, Dublin and Linda are evenweave fabrics with thread counts of 22, 25 and 27 respectively, and therefore can be replaced by other evenweave fabrics with the same thread counts.

Chapter 1
Getting started

Cross stitch is one of the easiest embroidery stitches to master and, with a little basic information, even a beginner will quickly be able to produce attractive results.

Fabrics

Cross stitch is generally worked on evenweave fabrics. These can vary in weight and texture through from finest linen to stiff canvas. Regular, even stitches are simple to work on these fabrics because they are made up of countable, equally-spaced threads.

Evenweave: The number of threads there are to 2.5 cm (1 in) of fabric determines the 'count' of the fabric. Thus, an 18-count fabric has more threads to 2.5 cm (1 in) than

an 11-count, and will be used for finer stitching. The most popular evenweave fabrics, especially for a beginner, are those that have threads woven together in blocks, so that individual threads do not have to be counted. These fabrics are called Aida and are available in different counts and in a wide range of colours.

Other evenweave fabrics, such as Linda and Oslo used in this book, have threads which are finer but are still easy to count. Cross stitches are generally worked over two or three threads in each direction, depending on how fine a result is required.

When working on all evenweave fabrics, it is important not to pull the stitches too tightly, as this will create holes in the fabric between the stitches.

Canvas is available in different types and mesh sizes and is mainly used for working with wool. The waste canvas method enables counted cross stitch to be worked on fabrics without a countable weave.

Cross stitch designs can be worked on any evenweave fabric, with a variety of yarns. Fabrics designed mainly for cross stitch are also available with different thread counts.

*(See **Getting started** page 18 for how to use waste canvas)*

Threads

There are various types of thread suitable for cross stitch embroidery. All are easy to work with and the following have been used for the projects in this book.

Stranded cotton: This is a six-stranded divisible thread. Any number of the strands can be used, depending on how fine the piece of embroidery is to be, and the count of the chosen fabric.

Flower thread: This is a single, non-divisible thread suitable for quite fine stitching and gives a matt finish.

Perlé cotton: This is a twisted, non-divisible thread which is highly mercerised to give it a rich sheen. It has only been used to make the tassels which decorate the needle case

and pincushion in **Small gifts** page 78, but this thread is suitable for all types of embroidery, including counted cross stitch.

Medici wool: This is a fine 2-ply wool particularly suitable for crewel embroidery and other fine, delicate work. Two strands may be used together in the needle.

Tapestry wool: This is a non-divisible, 4-ply wool used for canvaswork. Some colours are available in very large skeins, so are suitable for working backgrounds, as on the curtain tie-backs in **Gifts for the home** page 50.

Working with threads: Threads should be used in lengths of not more than 46 cm (18 in). If too long a piece is cut, the strands of divisible threads will be difficult to separate, and all threads will tend to twist and tangle. In addition, wools will fray as they are pulled through canvas, so use short lengths and start a new piece before this happens.

Tools and equipment

Besides basic sewing equipment required for making-up the cross stitch gifts, you will need the following:

Needles: Tapestry needles are the most suitable for stitching on evenweave fabrics since they have blunt ends which will not split the fabric threads. Needles are available in several sizes. The higher the number the finer the needle.

Crewel embroidery needles have sharp ends and are needed for stitching on fine fabrics which do not have countable threads. These, too, are available in different sizes and, as with other needles, the higher the number the larger the needle.

With both types of needle, the size you choose will depend both on the thickness of the thread you are using and the count of the fabric, thus a larger needle will be needed for working in wool on canvas than for working with stranded cotton on fine Aida fabric.

Scissors: You will need to be equipped with two types of scissors. Firstly, you will need large dressmaking scissors for cutting your fabrics to size, and for the various processes used in making up your gifts.

Secondly, when stitching the embroidery it is important to have a good pair of sharp embroidery scissors with fine points which will cut threads without 'chewing them up'.

Do not be tempted to use the scissors for anything other than embroidery and make sure that they cut right at the tip as this will make unpicking mistakes less traumatic. Finally, if you live in a house like mine, hide your scissors away – if they get near paper and glue they will no longer be of any use to you for needlework!

Hoops and frames: The purpose of hoops and frames is to hold the fabric taut so that stitches can be worked with an even tension and so prevent the fabric from puckering or distorting. It is advisable to work all evenweave fabrics, however small the design, in a hoop or frame.

When working on canvas, the choice of whether or not to use a frame is a personal one. Since cross stitch is worked in both directions, it exerts an even pull and does not distort the canvas, and a little practice will ensure that the wool is not pulled too tight. I enjoy stitching curled up on the sofa and find it more comfortable to work without a bulky frame. If you choose to work in this way too, bind the edges of your canvas with masking tape before you begin, to prevent the wools being snagged, and roll your work up after a session of stitching.

Working with a hoop: An embroidery hoop consists of two rings which fit inside each other. The larger ring has an adjustable screw, so that the fabric can be held taut.

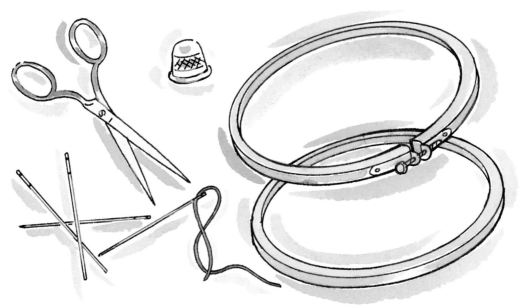

Hoops are inexpensive and are available in a variety of sizes. You will find that three basic sizes – small, medium and large – will meet all the needs of this book.

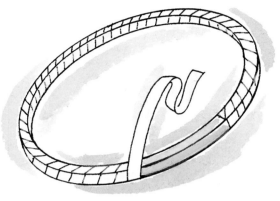

Before using a new hoop, bind both rings with cotton tape to prevent damage to the fabric and to help to prevent it loosening as you stitch.

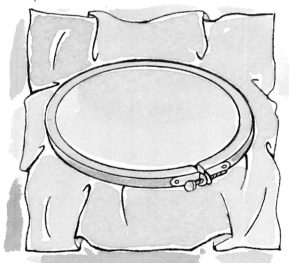

To use a hoop, lay the fabric right side up over the smaller ring, then gently ease the larger ring over the top. Adjust the screw so that the fabric is held firmly. Loosen the screw and remove both hoops if the work is to be left for any time. If the hoop is not large enough to encompass the whole design, move the hoop as stitching progresses. The stitches will not be damaged if the hoop is eased on and off gently and removed at the end of a session of stitching.

When working with a hoop or a frame, stitch with a stabbing motion, passing the needle through the fabric and pulling the whole length of the thread through to one side before passing the needle back in the other direction.

Working with a frame: A simple rotating frame is easy to use and can be bought in a variety of sizes according to your needs. The construction consists of two horizontal rollers with webbing attached. These slot into two upright arms which are held firmly in place with wing nuts.

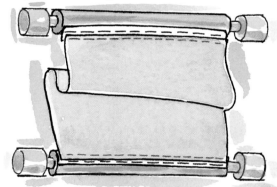

To set up your frame, first bind the edges of the canvas with masking tape. Then stitch the top and bottom edges of the canvas to the webbing, matching the centre of the canvas to the centre of the webbing.

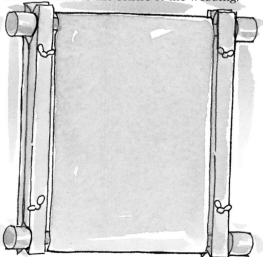

Slot the ends of the rollers into the grooves in the upright arms and rotate them until the canvas is taut. Tighten the wing nuts to hold the rollers firmly in place.

Working from a chart

The coloured charts in this book are very easy to follow. There is a key on each to tell you which colours are indicated; each coloured square represents one cross stitch. The instructions which accompany each project will tell you how many threads or woven fabric blocks should be covered by each complete cross stitch, and also where on the fabric to position the design.

How to adapt a chart: Adapting a chart is made easy by the use of squared tracing paper, which can be obtained from specialist needlecraft and art shops. It is available in various counts or squares to the centimetre (or inch). Choose the count that matches most nearly the count of the fabric on which you are going to be working. Should you be unable to find squared tracing paper, photocopy graph paper onto tracing paper.

Use either coloured pencils or felt-tipped pens when working out the design. I prefer to use the former as the inevitable mistakes can be rubbed out and put right.

The different elements of the design being adapted can be charted separately and then cut out and assembled in position on another sheet. Use the charts in this book in the same way to create new designs.

How to reverse a chart: To do this, copy it onto squared tracing paper with coloured pencils and then turn the tracing paper over – the chart will show through perfectly.

How to start and finish

It may be tempting to start with a knot but never do so! A knot may show through on the right side and spoil the look of the finished embroidery. A knot may also pull through the weave of the fabric or come undone, causing the work to unravel. Instead, when starting to stitch a new piece of work, leave an 8 cm (3 in) length of thread at the back of the work, which can later be darned into the back of the stitching. If you are starting a new piece of thread on fabric that is already partially stitched, secure the thread by running it through the back of two or three stitches. Make a small back stitch over another thread and bring the needle out in the correct position on the right side.

Finish off your thread in the same way and cut it close to the fabric.

The stitches

There are several methods of working cross stitch, but whichever you choose, the top stitch of the cross should always lie in the same direction.

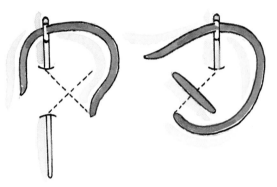

Cross stitch: Illustration A shows cross stitch being worked singly, each cross being completed before moving on to the next. Use this method for working small areas or single stitches of one colour.

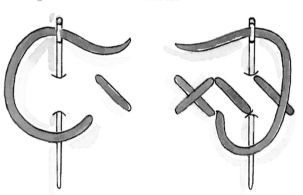

Illustration B shows a row of cross stitch being worked in two stages. First, a row of diagonal stitches is worked from right to left and then the crosses are completed by a second row of diagonal stitches worked in the opposite direction.

This method is used when covering a large area in one colour. It is also useful, when working lettering, as you can travel out on to the arm of a letter and then return in the opposite direction, ending up back at the main body of the letter.

When working groups of cross stitch in one colour, do not carry the thread across the back of the fabric to another group, as it is likely that the thread could show through as an unsightly line.

This design, worked in wool, shows how cross stitch can create rich and sumptuous effects.

Stem stitch: Stem stitch is an outline stitch, but it gives a thicker line than back stitch or Holbein stitch. It can follow the line of a curve well. Stem stitch is worked left to right, with the thread kept to the right of the needle. The stitches should be kept an even length and the needle should be inserted each time on the line to be covered. A thicker line will result if the needle is inserted slightly to the side of the line.

French knots: These are single stitches which can be used close together to give texture and shading, or scattered to add raised detail on top of an area already covered by another stitch such as cross stitch. The thickness of the thread used will dictate the size of the knot.

To make a French knot, bring the thread through to the right side of the fabric and hold it taut across the surface with the other hand. Twist the needle several times round the thread. Still holding the thread taut with the other hand, turn the needle round and take it back through the fabric next to where it first emerged.

Suitable lighting

Now you are ready to begin. Make sure that you work in a good light. I sometimes wonder how womens' eyesight survived the long hours spent at their needlework before the invention of the electric light bulb. A good light is especially important when working on dark fabrics or with dark-coloured threads. Daylight light bulbs are widely available and these offer a light in which it is possible to choose and match colours accurately. I would always prefer to work in real daylight, but when this is not possible, these bulbs are a good alternative.

Back stitch: Back stitch makes a solid line which is useful for outlining shapes to give them definition and for adding detail to a design. Work the stitch from left to right, keeping the stitches an even size.

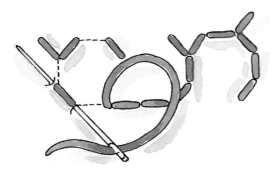

Holbein stitch: Also called double running stitch, Holbein stitch also makes a solid line on the right side of the work, but it appears the same on both sides of the fabric.

It is the stitch traditionally used in Assisi work and is worked in two stages. First work a row of even running stitches along the line of the design. Return with a second row of running stitches filling in the spaces.

Special techniques

How to use dressmaker's carbon paper:
Dressmaker's carbon paper is useful for transferring embroidery designs onto fabric. It is available from dress fabric and haberdashery departments in several colours including white.

1 Place the design or shape which is to be transferred in the correct place on the fabric, and secure it in position with small pieces of masking tape.
2 Slip a sheet of carbon under the design with the ink side down.
3 Using a sharp pencil, draw over the lines to transfer them to the fabric. (Always use a sharp pencil, as a blunt one will leave too thick a line.) Also, make sure that you have no rings on the hand holding the pencil, as these might make marks through the carbon where your hand is resting.
4 Remove the carbon carefully so as not to smudge any ink onto the fabric.

How to use waste canvas:
The use of waste canvas enables cross stitch to be worked on fabrics which do not have a coarse enough weave for the threads to be counted. The canvas is available in several counts or mesh sizes and, as with evenweave fabrics, the fewer threads to the cm (in) the larger the stitches will be.

1 Cut a piece of the appropriate canvas large enough to take the whole design.

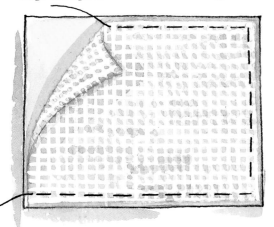

2 Tack (baste) the canvas firmly in position on the fabric. Stitch all round the edges of the canvas and, if the piece is large, stitch across diagonally as well. You can remove these diagonal lines as the embroidery progresses.

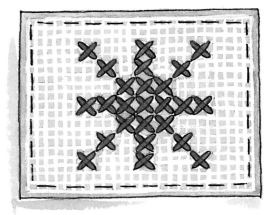

3 Work the cross stitch over the canvas using a crewel needle, working each cross over a single intersection of canvas threads.

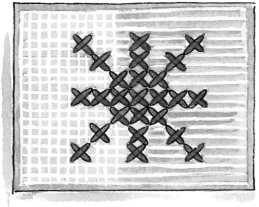

4 When the design has been embroidered, remove any remaining tacking (basting) threads.
5 Place the work face up on a towel and moisten the canvas with a damp cloth.
6 When the canvas threads have softened, remove them one at a time, first in one direction and then in the other.
7 Allow the work to dry slightly and then press carefully on the wrong side with the embroidery face down on a clean soft towel.

> *Note: The waste canvas method of working cross stitch gives you a great deal of flexibility for working designs on a range of fabrics that would otherwise be too finely woven to consider.*

Pressing the finished embroidery:

It is important when pressing your finished work that the stitches do not become crushed and flattened. To avoid this, put a thick, soft, white towel on the ironing board. Place the work face down on the towel and cover it with a clean white cloth. Press lightly with a warm iron. Your work will then be ready to make up as you wish.

Cross stitch worked on canvas can be pressed in the same way. The canvas will not be distorted as the stitches are worked in both directions and so exert an even pull. There is therefore no need to go to the trouble of stretching or blocking your work. Simply place the completed work face down on a clean, soft towel, lay a cloth over it and steam it lightly with the iron.

Sewing stitches
Slip stitch:

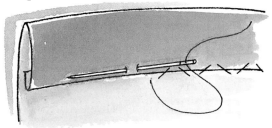

Slip stitch can be used for hems or for joining two folded edges together invisibly as when securing mitred corners.

To use slip stitch on a hem, secure the thread under the fold with a small back stitch. Slip the needle along inside the fold and then pick up a few threads of the fabric. To join two folded edges, slip the needle along inside each fold alternately.

Hem stitch:

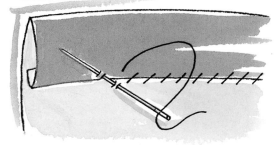

Secure the thread inside the fold of the hem with a small back stitch. Pick up a few threads of the fabric and then insert the needle diagonally up through the fold a little further on. Make the stitches in one movement and space them evenly.

Top stitching:

Top stitching simply refers to a line of stitching worked on the right side of the fabric, either for decoration or to secure a seam in place. A fairly large stitch is often chosen and this can be worked with special top stitching thread, which is a little thicker than normal sewing thread. You can use the presser foot on the machine as a guide to keep the line of stitching straight if it is worked close to an edge.

Sewing techniques

For all these operations a very sharp pair of scissors is essential, especially for neatening and finishing seams and curves. It is far easier to make precision cuts, and to avoid snipping the stitches if the scissors are sharp right up to their points.

Making a double hem:

A double hem is one in which the first fold is the same width as the second fold. This makes a firm edging and can be used for fine materials. First fold over half the hem allowance and press.

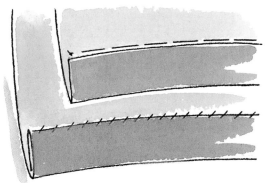

Fold over the same amount again with the raw edge close to the second fold. Press, pin and tack (baste) the hem, and then hem stitch with small even stitches.

Using bias binding:

Bias binding is cut on the cross and can therefore be used to bind curved as well as straight edges, as it will 'give' to accommodate the curve smoothly.

Ready-made bias binding is available in various colours, but if you cannot find the exact shade you want, it is an easy matter to make your own. It is often preferable to do this, as this way you can choose exactly the colour and quality fabric you require.

Making bias binding:

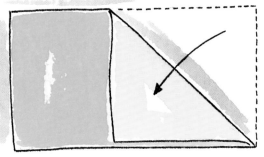

1 Lay your fabric flat and make a diagonal fold at an angle of 45° to the selvage. Cut along this fold.

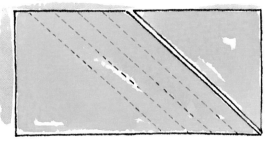

2 Decide how wide the binding is to be and allow 6 mm (¼ in) extra each side for turnings. Starting at the cut edge, use a ruler and water-soluble pen to mark parallel lines on the fabric to this measurement. Cut along these lines.

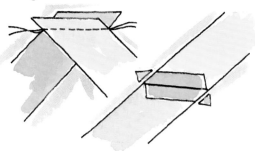

3 Join bias strips together by placing two strips at right angles, with right sides together, so that the threads are parallel. Pin and machine a narrow seam. Press the seam open and trim off the protruding corners. Fold and press a 6mm (¼ in) turning down each long edge.

Binding a raw edge with bias binding:

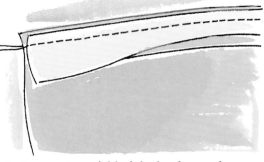

1 Open out one fold of the binding and, with right sides of fabric together, place the fabric and the bias binding edge to edge. Pin, tack (baste) and machine-stitch using the fold as a guide for stitching.

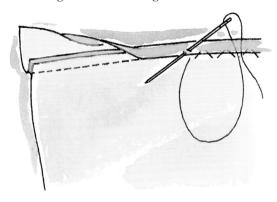

2 Fold the binding over to the wrong side of the fabric so that the raw edge is enclosed. Pin in position and slip stitch along the machined line.

Trimming seams:
All seam turnings should be trimmed to reduce their bulk. The turnings on a straight seam need to be trimmed to about 6 mm (¼ in). If the fabric is thick, trim one seam allowance slightly more than the other so there will be no ridge showing through on the right side.

> **Note:** *It is always worthwhile taking extra care with these sewing techniques, as well executed details such as evenly-trimmed seams, neatly stitched bindings and crisp, mitred corners give a professional-looking finish to a piece of work.*

Clipping curves:

If the curve is concave, simply clip the fabric at intervals, cutting to the stitching but taking care not to snip the thread. If the curve is convex, cut V-shaped notches in the turnings. This is done so that the outer edge of the turnings, which is longer than the seam line, will lie flat when the seam is turned and pressed.

Clipping corners:

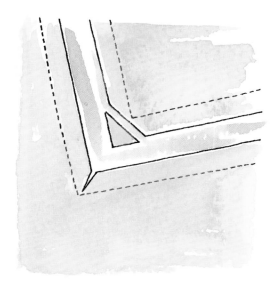

If an inside corner is to be clipped, cut diagonally just to the stitching. For an outside corner, trim off the corner diagonally across both seam allowances.

How to mitre a corner:

1 Fold and press the hem. Open out the hem and fold the corner over so that the diagonal crease runs through the point where the two pressed hemlines meet.

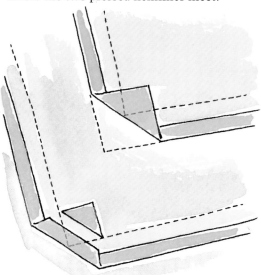

2 Trim off the corner about 6 mm (¼ in) from the diagonal crease.

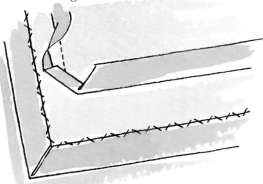

3 Re-fold along the pressed hemline in both directions, making sure that the diagonal folds of the mitre meet neatly. Press, pin and stitch the hem. Slip stitch the two diagonal folds together.

Using zip fasteners:

Zip fasteners have a variety of applications, and there are several ways to insert them. For the purposes of this book I have used a very simple method.

Most sewing machines have a zipper foot attachment which makes it possible to machine quite close to the teeth of the zip.

Inserting a zip:

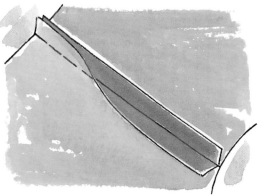

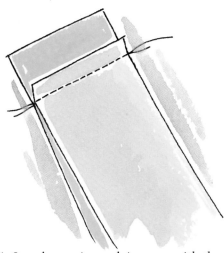

1 With right sides together, tack (baste) the seam in which the zip is to be inserted. Press the turnings open.

1 Start by sewing a plain seam with the right sides together. Trim one seam allowance only to 6 mm (¼ in)
2 Press the seam so that the trimmed allowance is covered by the untrimmed one.

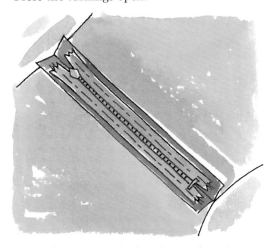

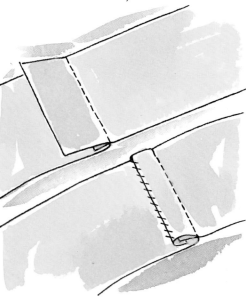

2 On the wrong side, lay the zip face down so that the teeth lie along the tacked (basted) seam line. Pin and tack (baste) the zip in position along each side of the teeth.
3 Turn the fabric over so that the right side is facing up, and unpick the tacked (basted) seam. Open the zip and machine half the left-hand side, keeping the edge of the zipper foot an even distance from the teeth. Stop machining with the needle in the fabric, raise the foot and close the zip. Lower the foot and machine to the end.
4 Repeat for the right-hand side.

Making a flat felled seam:
This is a strong seam which encloses all raw edges and is suitable for reversible fabrics, since either side of the finished seam can be the right side.

3 Turn-in the raw edge of the untrimmed allowance and hem it neatly in position, or machine stitch close to the fold.

Mounting and framing
After hours spent stitching a sampler or picture, it is worth the time and expense to frame it well. A carefully chosen frame will enhance the work and show it up to its full advantage. But, however beautiful the frame, the embroidery will look less than perfect if it is not first properly laced onto

stiff mounting board to keep it taut and eliminate any wrinkles. Most framers will do this for you, but you could easily do it yourself and so save some money.

Lacing the fabric over mounting board:

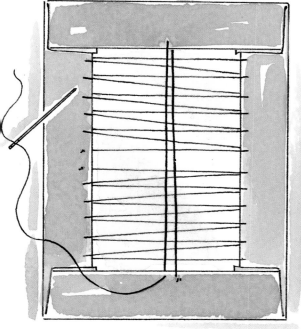

1 Cut a piece of mounting board the size and shape required for the finished picture, adding a little extra all round to allow for the overlap of the frame.
2 Place the board centrally on the back of the embroidery.
3 Fold the top and bottom edges of the fabric over the board. Push a pin into the board at the centre of each edge to secure the fabric.
4 Check that the embroidery is in the right position and that the threads of the fabric are straight with the edge of the board.
5 Thread a long darning needle with strong thread and make a large knot at the end.
6 Starting at the centre and working outwards, lace the top and bottom edges together pulling the fabric taut. Check continually that the fabric threads are straight with the edge of the board.
7 Lace the side edges together in the same way, folding-in the corners neatly.
8 When all the lacing is complete, tighten all the stitches and secure the thread ends by knotting them tightly as at the start.

Choosing frames:

Your work is now ready for framing. There is no doubt that a custom-made, conventional picture frame is best. There are cheaper alternatives, such as clip frames, but these crush the stitches and let in the dust and grime.

Some people feel that glass obscures the stitches, but I think that this effect is minimal and that the need to protect the work from dust outweighs this slight risk. I usually use non-reflective glass, which, though slightly more expensive, avoids the reflections which make it difficult to get a clear view of the work.

This style of traditional cross stitch border makes a frame in itself, and could be used to edge a design, as a frame within a frame.

Chapter 2
Gifts for the kitchen

Scandinavian table linen set

In days gone by, table linen was invariably home-made and hand embroidered, and often formed part of a young bride's trousseau. Such items were often handed down from one generation to another to become family heirlooms, and I have included this project in the hope that it may become just such a treasured gift.

The design is influenced by traditional Scandinavian cross stitch patterns which are often worked in a single colour on a white background. The eight-pointed star is a motif that is frequently used, as are hearts and birds. The 'tree of life' symbol in the centre of the borders occurs in many forms and in many countries.

REQUIREMENTS
For the tablecloth:
*(The finished size of the tablecloth is
    134 x 134 cm (52½ x 52½ in) square)*
*Oslo 22 count evenweave fabric
    (Zweigart E3947) in White, 150 x 150 cm
    (59 x 59 in) square*
*DMC stranded cotton – 9 skeins of
    number 349*
For each napkin:
*A piece of Oslo 48 x 48 cm (19 x 19 in)
    square*
DMC stranded cotton number 349
*(When cutting the squares for the napkins,
    pull out threads of the fabric at the
    correct measurements as a cutting guide)*
For each napkin ring:
*A piece of Oslo 25 x 25 cm (10 x 10 in)
    square*
DMC stranded cotton number 349
Small embroidery hoop
Soft iron-on interfacing
Red satin bias binding
Red sewing thread
For the set:
Tapestry needle size 26
Large embroidery hoop.
Dark tacking (basting) thread
Dressmaking pins
Sewing needle
White thread
Tacking (basting) thread
*(See **Getting started** page 21 for how to
mitre corners, page 19 for how to make a
double hem, page 19 for slip stitch, page 19
for hem stitch, and page 20 for making bias
binding, joining bias binding, and binding a
raw edge)*

Stitching the tablecloth:
1 With the dark tacking (basting) thread, tack (baste) along the centre line of the fabric in both directions. Where the lines cross will mark the centre of the tablecloth. (Use the threads of the fabric as a guide to keep the tacking (basting) line straight.)
2 Position the centre of the base of the 'tree of life' motif 27 cm (10⅝ in) from the centre point of the tablecloth. Place the fabric in the embroidery hoop and begin stitching at this point, using two strands of thread throughout and forming each cross over two threads in each direction.
3 Follow the chart and move the hoop as you proceed until one side of the square is completed. Work the corner and continue with the next side. Proceed in this way until the square is completed.
4 Press the work lightly on the wrong side with the embroidery face down on a clean soft towel.

Making up the tablecloth:
1 Make a single turning to the wrong side 36 cm (14 in) from the lower edge of the embroidered border.
2 Trim the turnings to 4 cm (1½ in) and fold a double hem 2 cm (¾ in) deep.
3 Tack (baste) the hem, mitring the corners.
4 Using white thread, slip stitch the mitred corners and hem stitch the hem.
5 Remove all tacking (basting) threads and press on the wrong side.

Stitching the napkin border:
(As the border is stitched near the edge of the fabric it is not possible to use a hoop. While stitching, make sure not to pull the thread too tight.)
1 Work the border, stitching each cross over two threads and leaving two threads between each cross. Work the first side of the border 4 cm (1½ in) in from the edge of the fabric and to a length of 40 cm (15¾ in).
2 Count the number of crosses, and work the second side of the border to match. Proceed with the work in this way until the square is completed.
3 Press lightly on the wrong side.

Fresh red and white is a classic combination for a table linen set, and the birds and flowers, and pretty heart motifs epitomize Scandinavian design. This would make a wonderful gift.

Making up the napkins:
1 Remove a thread on each side 3 cm (1⅛ in) from the edge of the stitching. Trim the fabric to this line.
2 Press a double hem 1 cm (⅜ in) deep all round. (The hem should cover the wrong side of the embroidery.)
3 Mitre the corners; and pin and tack (baste) the hem.

4 Slip stitch the napkin corners and hem stitch the hem.
5 Remove the tacking (basting) threads and press lightly on the wrong side.

Stitching the napkin rings:
1 Making sure the design will be in the top half of the square of fabric, place it in the hoop and work the motif of your choice.

Follow the charts on these pages to work the Scandinavian table linen set. As the charts are so versatile you could, for example, use the tree of life and birds motif on its own, and adapt different parts of the design for other pieces of table linen or, of course, to decorate linen anywhere in the home.

2 As before, use two strands of thread and work each cross over two threads in each direction.
3 Remove the fabric from the hoop, and press lightly on the wrong side with the embroidery face down on a clean soft towel.

Making up the napkin ring:
1 Trim the embroidery to 5 cm x 16 cm (2 in x 6¼ in) making sure that the design is centred in this rectangle.
2 Cut a second piece the same size from the remaining fabric. This will be the lining of the napkin ring.
3 Iron the interfacing onto this piece.
4 With the right sides of the embroidered piece inside and the short edges together, join the short edges with a 1 cm (⅜ in) seam. Trim the turnings and press the seam open. Turn right side out.
5 Repeat with the lining piece, but do not turn right side out.

> *Note: If you would like to make a firmer napkin ring, or a slightly padded version, simply substitute a thicker interfacing, or another alternative would be to use some lightweight padding instead.*

6 Place the lining inside the embroidered ring, with wrong sides and seams together.
7 Cut two lengths of bias binding approximately 20 cm (8 in) long. Join each to form a circle to fit the napkin ring edge.

8 Bind the edges, matching the edge of the binding to the edge of the napkin ring. As the ring is so small it is easier to handsew the binding with a small running stitch before turning to the inside to hem stitch.

Pot holders

One of the first gifts I ever made as a small girl at school was a cross stitch pot holder. My mother put it carefully away among her treasures and it was never actually used. These two pot holders, whilst being attractive enough to hang on the kitchen wall, are also designed to be practical, being made of washable fabrics and heat insulated.

REQUIREMENTS
For each pot holder:
11 count Aida evenweave fabric (Zweigart E1007 colour number 101-Antique white) 25 x 25 cm (10 x 10 in) square
Tapestry needle size 26
Embroidery hoop
DMC stranded cottons: for the hen, one skein each black, red 349, and grey 647; for the cockerel, one skein each black and red 349
1 m (1 yd) black bias binding 2.5 cm (1 in) wide
25 x 25 cm (10 x 10 in) square of washable black fabric such as velvet or wool mixture
50 cm x 25 cm (19½ x 10 in) piece of insulating fabric such as old washed blanket
Dressmaker's pins
Tacking (basting) thread
Sewing needle
Black thread for machine sewing
*(See **Getting started** page 20 for binding a raw edge)*

Stitching the embroidery:
1 Place the square of Aida in the embroidery hoop and follow the chart, using three strands of thread throughout and stitching each cross over one block of threads.
2 Remove the work from the hoop and, with the stitching face down, press lightly on the wrong side, on a soft clean towel.

Making up the pot holders:
1 Trim the Aida fabric to 3 cm (1⅛ in) from the edge of the embroidery.
2 Cut one piece of black backing fabric and two pieces of insulating material to the same size as the Aida fabric.
3 Place the backing fabric and embroidered Aida together with right sides out, and sandwich the insulating fabric between. Tack (baste) through all layers diagonally,

and then again, 1 cm (⅜ in) from the edge of the embroidery.

Making the hanging loop:
1 Cut a length of bias binding 14 cm (5½ in) long. Fold it in half lengthways and machine edges together. Press well.

2 Fold the loop in half and place it in the centre of the back top edge of the pot holder, with the loop pointing into the centre. Tack (baste) firmly in place.

Finishing the pot holder:
1 With right sides together, pin the bias binding to the front of the pot holder, placing the edge of the binding two thread blocks in from the edge of the Aida fabric. Join the binding to fit.
2 Tack and machine stitch using the fold of the bias binding as a stitching guide.
3 Turn the binding to the back of the pot holder to enclose raw edges, and slip stitch over the machine stitches.
4 Pull up the loop and stitch it into place.

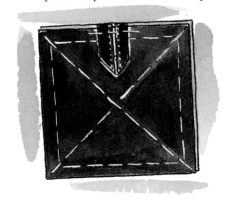

The cock and hen motifs make these pot holders into real kitchen classics, and a gift that anyone with a graphic eye would appreciate.

	647		349		B

Cherry gâteau apron

Whenever I look through cookery books, my eye is always drawn to photographs of luscious but forbidden gâteaux and pastries, with their lashings of cream and piles of fruit. I seldom bake such extravagant concoctions, but I have designed this apron as a reminder of the more frivolous aspects of cooking, and to bring a smile to the hours spent on more mundane kitchen tasks.

REQUIREMENTS
*1 m (1 yd) 122 cm (48 in) wide navy
    100% cotton fabric
10 mesh waste canvas 20 x 20 cm (8 x 8 in)
    square
Tacking (basting) thread
Sewing needle
Crewel embroidery needle size 7
Large embroidery hoop
DMC stranded cottons – one skein of each
    colour as indicated on the chart
3 m (3¼ yd) navy satin bias binding
Dressmaker's pins
Metric squared pattern guide paper
Tracing paper
Pencil
Light coloured chalk pencil
Navy thread for sewing machine
(See **Getting started** page 17 for stem stitch,
page 18 for using waste canvas, page 21 for
clipping curves, page 20 for joining bias
binding, page 20 for binding a raw edge and
page 19 for top stitching)*

Stitching the embroidery:
1 Cut a piece of navy fabric approximately 35 cm (13½ in) square.
2 Tack (baste) the waste canvas in the centre, and mount it in the hoop.
3 Stitch the design, following the chart, and forming each cross over one intersection of canvas threads. Use three strands of thread for the cross stitch and four for the stem stitched cherry stalks.
4 When the embroidery is complete, remove the waste canvas, allow the fabric to dry a little and then press it on the wrong side, with the work face down on a soft, clean towel.

Making up the patch pocket:
1 Draw up the shape of the pocket on squared pattern guide paper. Trace it onto tracing paper and cut out.

2 Pin the traced pattern over the cake embroidery, so that the design sits comfortably in the space below the fold line. Pin it in place.
3 On the fabric, draw round the pattern with the chalk pencil and cut out, leaving an extra 1 cm (⅜ in) all round for turnings.
4 Press a 1cm (⅜ in) turning to the wrong side at the top. Machine stitch.

5 Turn the top edge to the outside of the pocket along the fold line to form the pocket facing. Stitch the facing in place along the seam line on each side. Trim the top corners and the seam allowances, clip curves up to the seam line.

6 Turn the facing to the inside of the pocket and press. Press the seam allowance to the wrong side and tack (baste).

Making up the apron:
1 Draw up the shape of the apron on squared pattern paper, and cut it out.
2 Fold the navy fabric and place the centre front edge of the pattern to the fold. Pin the pattern to the fabric and cut it out.

3 Remove the pattern and bind the edge of the apron with satin bias binding, placing the edge of the binding to the edge of the fabric. Join the binding to fit.

Attaching the pocket to the apron:
1 Fold the apron in half from top to bottom to find the centre.
2 Place the centre of the pocket to the centre of the apron, with the top of the pocket 6 cm (2½ in) from the top of the apron. Pin and tack (baste) the pocket in place securely.
3 Top stitch close to the edge of the pocket, strengthening the top corners with a double line of stitching.

Making the strap and ties:
1 From the remaining fabric, cut one strip 6 x 56 cm (2⅜ x 22 in) and two strips 6 x 65 cm (2⅜ x 25 in).

This mouth-watering design would be a perfect gift for anyone with a sweet tooth, and would be an inspiration to an aspiring cook.

2 Turn and press 0.5 cm (¼ in) turnings to the wrong side all round each strip.
3 Fold the strips in half lengthways with turnings inside. Pin, tack (baste) and top stitch close to the edge all round.
4 Attach each end of the short strip to the top of the apron, and the long strips to the sides for ties.

> **Note:** *If you do not want to make your own apron, you could stitch the design on to a bought one. In this case, find the centre of the apron and attach the waste canvas so that the embroidery will fall in the desired place.*

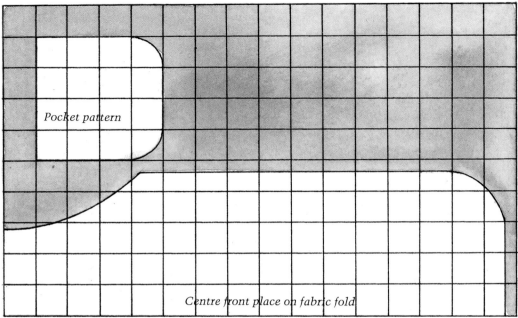

Pocket pattern

Centre front place on fabric fold

1 square = 5 cm (2 in)

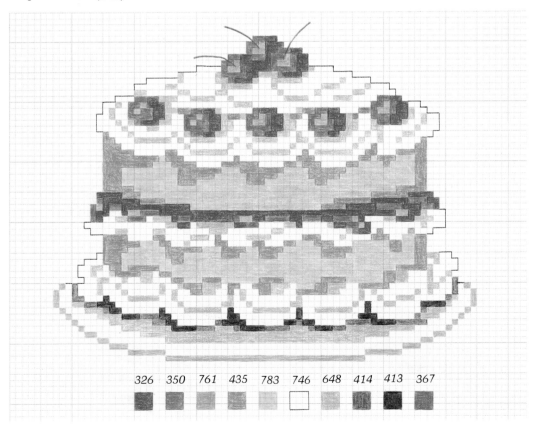

| 326 | 350 | 761 | 435 | 783 | 746 | 648 | 414 | 413 | 367 |

Calico shopping bag

The botanical drawings and lithographs of past centuries are a wonderful source of inspiration for cross stitch designs because of their clearly defined details. The design for this shopping bag came from a lithograph dated 1876. The Latin name for Garden Pea has been added in the manner of botanical studies of that period.

Whether kept to treasure, or well used, this design will always retain its freshness.

*1 metre unbleached calico 140 cm
(55 in) wide.
10 mesh waste canvas 17 x 21 cm
(6½ x 8 in)
14 mesh waste canvas 6 x 14 cm
(5½ x 2 ins)
Dark tacking (basting) thread
Sewing needle
Crewel embroidery needle size 7
25 cm (10 in) embroidery hoop
DMC stranded cottons – one skein of each
colour as indicated on the chart
Ivory thread for machine sewing
Tracing paper
Ruler and pencil
Sticky tape
Dressmaker's carbon paper
(See* **Getting started** *page 17 for stem stitch,
page 18 for using waste canvas, page 18 for
using dressmaker's carbon paper and page
19 for working top stitch)*

Preparing and cutting the fabric:

1 As calico shrinks considerably, wash the fabric before use. After washing, press while still damp to remove all creases.

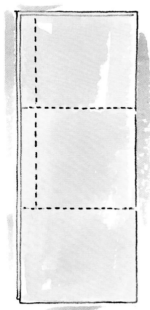

2 Fold fabric lengthways, cut edges together, and cut two pieces 44 cms (17¼ in) wide, 46 cms (18 in) deep. (These pieces will form the outer embroidered bag and lining. The remaining fabric is used for the strap.)

Stitching the embroidery:

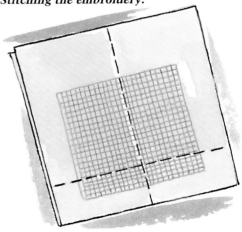

1 Open out one piece of fabric and stitch a line of tacking (basting) down the centre to the fold line. Tack (baste) a second line horizontally 13 cms (5 in) from the fold line. These form a guide for positioning the design.

2 Tack (baste) the piece of 10 mesh waste canvas in position over the centre and base-tacked (basted) lines.

3 Place the fabric in the embroidery hoop and work the design, placing the base of the stalk on the base line and matching the centre of the design to the centre of the fabric. Using three strands of thread and the crewel needle and working each cross over one intersection of canvas threads, work only the peas at this stage.

4 When the peas are complete, remove the waste canvas and tacking (basting) threads. Press the fabric face down on a clean towel while still damp.

5 Using a ruler and pencil, draw a rectangle 12 x 20.5 cm (4¾ x 8 in) on tracing paper. Draw a line across the rectangle 4.5 cm (1¾ in) up from the lower edge.

6 Place the tracing centrally over the peas and attach it to the fabric with sticky tape. Slip the carbon paper under the tracing, ink side down, and transfer the rectangle on to the fabric by drawing over the lines with a pencil. Remove the carbon and tracing.

7 Mark the centre of the lettering space with a tacking (basting) thread.

8 Tack (baste) the piece of 14 mesh waste canvas into place over the lettering space, making sure that the canvas threads are in line with the lines of the traced rectangle.

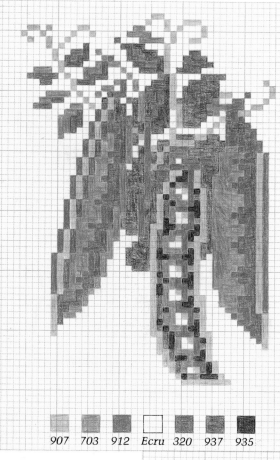

| 907 | 703 | 912 | Ecru | 320 | 937 | 935 |

9 Place the fabric in the embroidery hoop and work the lettering following the chart and using two strands of colour 935. Stitch each cross over one intersection of canvas threads. Match the centre of the lettering to the tacked (basted) centre line and sit the letters 1 cm (⅜ in) up from the base line of the rectangle.

10 Remove the waste canvas and press the work lightly on the wrong side.

11 Replace the fabric in the embroidery hoop and work the stem stitch border using two strands of colour number 935.

12 Remove the fabric from the hoop and press it lightly on the wrong side, with the work face down on a clean soft towel.

Making up the bag:

1 Fold the embroidered piece with the right side inside. Machine the side seams 14 cm (5½ in) from the sides of the embroidered rectangle. Trim the turnings, clip the lower corners, turn right side out and press.

2 Repeat with the lining piece, but making it slightly smaller, and leaving it with the wrong side out.

3 Make a fold to the wrong sides of the bag and lining 40 cms (15¾ in) from the base and press. Trim turnings to 2.5 cm (1 in).

4 Insert the lining into the bag with wrong sides together. Pin the folded edges together at the top.

Making the handle and finishing the bag:

1 Open out the remaining fabric. Cut one piece the full width of the fabric and 14 cm (5½ in) wide.

2 Fold and press 1.5 cm (⅝ in) turnings down each long side. Trim the turnings to 0.5 cm (¼ in).

3 Fold lengthwise with the turnings inside and press. Pin the folded edges together. Set the sewing machine to a long, straight stitch and top stitch close to the edge. Top stitch the other long side to match. Press well.

4 Insert each end of the strap between the bag and lining at the side seams.

5 Top stitch close to the edge through all layers at the top of the bag. Machine a line of stitching 2.5 cm (1 in) from the edge.

> **Note:** *This design of garden peas would also make an attractive picture to hang in the kitchen or in a garden room.*

Art Deco tray cloth

The bold and colourful ceramic designs of Clarice Cliff were the inspiration for this simple tray cloth. She brought to British pottery a new and uninhibited style of decoration which evokes the lively spirit of the 1920s and 30s. By restricting the design to the corner of the tray cloth, it can easily be applied to a fabric rectangle of any size so you could also use the motif to decorate a tablecloth or envelope-style bag.

To calculate the amount of fabric required, measure the width and depth of the tray or other surface and add at least 10 cm (4 in) all round for hems.

REQUIREMENTS
Oslo 22 count evenweave fabric (Zweigart
*   E3947) in Antique white (colour 101)*
Dark tacking (basting) thread
Sewing needle
Embroidery hoop
Tapestry needle size 26
DMC stranded cottons – one skein of each
*   colour indicated on the chart*
Dressmaker's pins
Matching thread
*(See **Getting started** page 17 for Holbein*
stitch, page 19 for making a double hem,
page 21 for mitring corners, page 19 for slip
stitch and page 19 for hem stitch)

Preparing the fabric:
1 Measure the tray and mark the finished size of the cloth with a rectangle of tacked (basted) lines. Stitch the lines of tacking (basting) along a thread of the fabric in order to keep them straight.
2 In the top right-hand corner mark the position for the design by running a short line of tacking (basting) stitches 5 cm (2 in) in from the top and right-hand marking threads. Count the number of threads to ensure that the embroidery will be evenly placed in the corner.
3 Mark the lower left-hand corner in the same way.

Stitching the embroidery:
1 Place the top right-hand corner of the prepared fabric in the embroidery hoop.
2 Using two strands of thread, work the cross stitch first, and then work the black lines in Holbein stitch. Stitch each cross over two threads in each direction, and work the Holbein stitch over two threads.

3 When the design is complete, move the embroidery hoop to the lower left-hand corner and work only the green and yellow lines of cross stitch and the line of black Holbein stitch.
4 Remove the work from the hoop and press it lightly on the wrong side with the work face down on a clean towel.

Making up the tray cloth:
1 Withdraw a thread in each direction 3 cm (1¼ in) from the tacked (basted) line which marks the finished size of the cloth. Cut along the line of the withdrawn thread.
2 Fold a double hem 1.5 cm (⅝ in) deep along the line of tacking (basting) thread. Mitre the corners and tack (baste) them.
3 Slip stitch the corners and hem-stitch the hem with small stitches.

The vibrant colours of the Art Deco style have a timeless appeal, and complement many modern ceramics surprisingly well.

4 Remove all tacking (basting) threads.
5 Using the yellow stranded cotton, work a row of Holbein stitch 1.5 cm (⅝ in) in from the edge of the tray cloth. Use the line of hem stitching as a guide.
6 Press the finished tray cloth lightly on the wrong side.

> **Note:** *This simple design could be used on the same fabric to decorate the corners of a tablecloth and matching napkins. It would also look good as a cross stitch picture mount, or on the corner of a fabric album cover.*

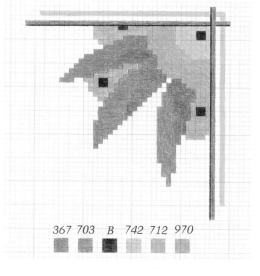

367 703 B 742 712 970

Ivy leaf shelf edging

Many kitchens have open shelves or dressers on which collections of china can be attractively displayed, and a pretty embroidered edging adds a finishing touch. This delicate repeat pattern of ivy leaves has been deliberately designed in muted shades of green so that it will compliment china that is either patterned or plain.

REQUIREMENTS
Aida band 5 cm (2 in) wide in ivory colour (Zweigart E7107). (To calculate the amount needed, measure the length of the shelf and add 3 cm (1¼ in) for turnings of 1.5 cm (⅝ in) at each end.)
DMC stranded cottons – one skein of each colour indicated on the chart will be sufficient to work two one-metre (39½ in) lengths of shelf edging
Tapestry needle size 26
Small embroidery hoop
Ivory cotton lace edging the same length as the Aida band
Ivory sewing thread
Sewing needle
Dressmaker's pins
Double-sided adhesive tape or self-adhesive fixing putty
(See **Getting started** *page 19 for making a double hem and page 19 for slip stitch)*

Working the embroidery:
1 Find the centre of the length of Aida band and mark it with a pin.
2 Place the fabric in the hoop and, using two strands of thread, work each cross over one woven thread block.
3 Starting at the centre of the design, work the repeat pattern from the middle

outwards, finishing the embroidery approximately 2.5 cm (1in) from each end.
4 Remove the work from the hoop and press it lightly on the wrong side with the embroidery face down on a clean towel.

Making up the shelf edging:
1 Fold and press a narrow double hem at each end. Slip stitch neatly.
2 Slip stitch the lace edging in place on the wrong side of the lower edge, turning in 1.5 cm (⅝ in) neatly at each end.
3 Press lightly again on the wrong side.
4 Attach the edging to the shelf with double-sided adhesive tape or small pieces of self-adhesive fixing putty.

This ivy leaf border design would look very attractive as a window blind edging, and could also be used to decorate table or bed linen.

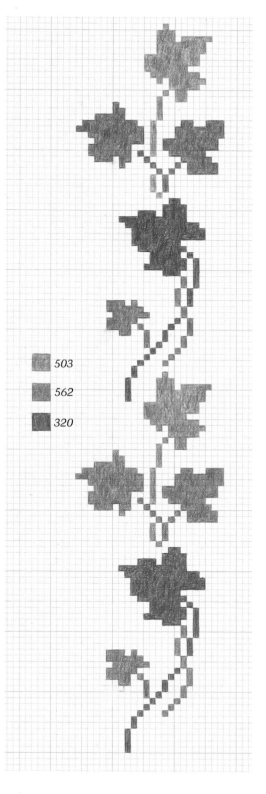

503

562

320

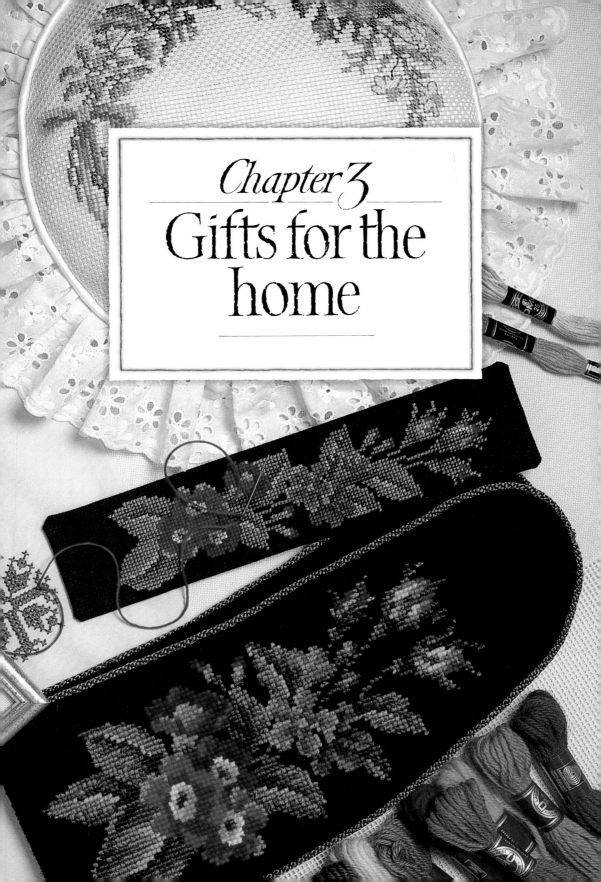

Chapter 3
Gifts for the home

Greek island bed linen

In bygone days, Greek girls began at a very early age to work embroideries in preparation for their weddings. They were required to make bed spreads, cushion covers, pillowcases, bed valances and other furnishings as well as decorative borders for skirts and under garments. Rich and varied styles developed in the different islands, and these traditions still persist today.

Cross stitch is among several stitches that were commonly used, as in this design taken from a Dodecanese bed valance dating from the late 17th century – an example of a delightful Greek tradition to decorate bed linen and bed hangings with embroideries.

The colours chosen for this design reflect its Greek origins. You could easily substitute your own colours to suit your decor.

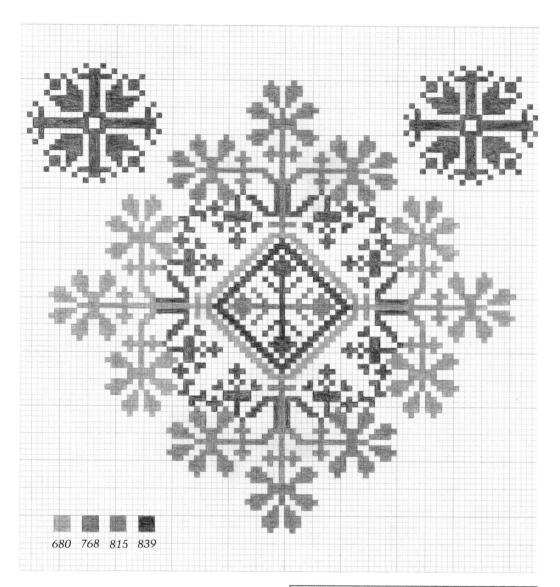

680 768 815 839

REQUIREMENTS
Plain cotton percale single duvet cover and
    matching pillowcase
50 cm (½ yd) 10 mesh waste canvas
Dark tacking (basting) thread and needle
Crewel embroidery needle size 7
DMC stranded cottons – colours as
    indicated on the chart. You will need
    one skein of brown 839 and three each of
    the other colours
Large embroidery hoop
Thread for sewing machine
(See **Getting started** page 18 for using waste
canvas)

Note: If you wish to work the embroidery
on a double duvet cover, work the
embroidery in two halves, placing a large
central motif in each half and working the
border of small motifs as before. For the
second pillowcase work the design so that
the border is stitched at the right-hand end
of the pillowcase. You could also decorate
towels, by working a line of motifs across
their woven bands. This would be ideal for
an en suite bathroom.

Preparing the duvet cover:
1 Unpick the top seam of the duvet cover.
2 Fold the cover in half lengthways, align the side seams, and lightly press the centre fold. Open out and run a line of tacking (basting) stitches along the centre line through a single layer of fabric for about 36 cm (14 in) from the top seam line. Also mark the unpicked seam line with a line of tacking (basting) stitches.
3 Cut a piece of waste canvas 24 cm (9½ in) square. Tack (baste) this firmly to the duvet cover, matching the centre of the canvas to the centre line on the cover and placing the top edge of the canvas 10 cm (4 in) from the seam line.
4 Cut two pieces of waste canvas 50 x 7.5 cm (19⅝ x 3 in). Tack (baste) one each side of the central piece of canvas, with the top edges 7 cm (2¾ in) from the seam line, and making sure that the horizontal threads of the canvas are in line.

Stitching the embroidery:
1 Work the large central motif, matching the centre of the motif to the centre of the cover and placing the top of the motif 12 cm (4¾ in) from the tacked (basted) seam line. Use three strands of thread in the needle and stitch each cross over one intersection of canvas threads.
2 Work the border of small motifs. Use the blue, ochre and maroon threads alternately and work the motifs 10 canvas threads apart, keeping them in line with one other.

Finishing the duvet cover:
1 Remove all the tacking (basting) threads except the one marking the seam line. Cut away the excess canvas between the motifs and remove the canvas.
2 Allow the fabric to dry slightly, then press the work on the wrong side with the embroidery face down on a clean, soft towel.
3 Turn the cover inside out and, with the right sides together, re-stitch the top seam and neaten raw edges.
4 Remove the tacking (basting) thread and turn right side out. Press well.

Preparing the pillowcase:
1 With the opening of the pillowcase to the right, unpick the top and bottom seams from the left-hand end to the centre.
2 Place the top and bottom seams together and lightly press the fold to find the centre.

Tack (baste) a line of stitches 20 cm (8 in) long on this line, starting at the left-hand side of the pillowcase and stitching through a single layer of fabric.
3 Cut a piece of waste canvas 42 x 9 cm (16½ x 3½ in).

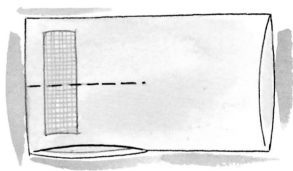

4 Match the centre of the canvas strip to the centre line of the pillowcase and tack (baste) in place with the edge of the canvas 4 cm (1½) from the left-hand end of the pillowcase.

Stitching the embroidery:
1 Work a row of five small motifs in alternate colours, as before. Place the centre of the middle motif on the tacked (basted) centre line and 6 cm (2⅜ in) from the left-hand end of the pillowcase.
2 As on the duvet cover, work the design motifs 10 canvas threads apart, using three strands of thread.

Finishing the pillowcase:
1 Cut away excess canvas between the motifs. Remove the waste canvas.
2 Allow the fabric to dry slightly, and press lightly on the wrong side with the work face down on a clean towel.
3 Turn inside out and re-stitch the top and bottom seams of the pillowcase.
4 Turn right side out and press well.

Fragrant sleep pillow

A small pillow, filled with gently fragrant herbs or pot pourri and placed beside an ordinary pillow, will not only soothe you to sleep, but perfume the bedroom as well.

A great variety of herbs and flowers can be used in this way, in combinations to suit your taste. Lavender, rose, camomile, marjoram and spearmint are shown in the embroidered spray. These are all traditional ingredients used to fill sleep pillows.

Alternatively, a floral pot pourri could be used, but take care not to choose one with a perfume that is too overpowering. Because the herbs or pot pourri are enclosed inside the pillow, their scent will last much longer than if they were exposed to the air in a bowl or dish.

Besides having therapeutic attractions, this pretty design could take pride of place on a bed, nestled amongst other decorative pillows.

REQUIREMENTS
11 count damask Aida evenweave fabric
(Zweigart E3238 number 264)
approximately 40 cm x 80 cm
(16 in x 32 in)
DMC stranded cottons – one skein of each
colour as indicated on the chart
Tapestry needle size 26
Large embroidery hoop
One sheet A3 tracing paper
Compass and pencil
2 m (2¼ yd) wide broderie anglaise
trimming in ivory to match Aida
Ivory machine thread
Tacking (basting) thread
Sewing needle
Dressmaking pins
25 cm (10 in) zip fastener
1 m (1 yd) piping cord size 2
1 m (1 yd) ivory satin bias binding
Plain cotton fabric for inner pad
30 cm x 60 cm (12 in x 24 in)
Polyester filling and mixed herbs or pot
pourri for filling
(See **Getting started** page 17 for working
back stitch, and page 22 for how to insert a
zip, page 20 for making and joining bias
binding, page 21 for clipping curves, and
page 22 for making a flat felled seam)

Stitching the embroidery:
1 Cut the Aida fabric in half to give two
pieces 40 cm (16 in) square.
2 Making sure that the design will be
positioned centrally on the fabric, put one of
the squares into the embroidery hoop.
3 Following the chart, stitch the work using
three strands of thread for the cross stitch
and two strands for the back stitch. Work
each cross over one block of threads.
4 When the embroidery is complete,
remove it from the hoop, and press lightly
on the wrong side, with the work face down
on a clean soft towel.
5 Using the compass, draw a 27 cm (10¾ in)
diameter circle on the tracing paper. Place
the tracing over the embroidery so that the
design is in the centre with equal space all
round. Pin the tracing paper to the fabric
and cut along the drawn line.

Making the cushion back:
1 Cut the second square of Aida in half to
give two pieces 40 cm x 20 cm (16 in x 8 in).
2 Press a 1.5 cm (⅝ in) turning down one
long side of each half.

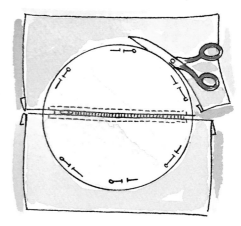

3 Place the two folded edges together and
insert the zip, placing it at an equal distance
from each edge of the fabric.
4 At the open end of the zip tack (baste) the
two folded edges together.
5 Place the tracing paper circle so that the
zip goes across the centre of the circle, pin
to the fabric and cut out.

Attaching the piping:
1 If using bought bias binding, press it flat.
If making your own, cut the bias strip 3 cm
(1¼ in) wide, but do not turn and press the
seam allowance.
2 Pin the bias strip to the embroidered
circle with right sides together and edges
matching. Fold the satin strip in half and
enclose the piping cord as you fold, placing
the pins close to the cord.

3 When you have almost pinned around the
circle in this way, join the bias strip, cut the
cord to the required length and enclose it.
4 Tack the piping firmly in place, and
machine stitch using the zipper foot to
stitch close to the cord. Remove the tacking
(basting) stitches.

367• 320 503 913 348 725 687 899 761 609 210 208 W

Attaching the frill:

1 Join the broderie anglaise trimming using a flat felled seam.

2 Starting with a large knot, run a gathering thread along the raw edge using small running stitches. Work the gathering stitches in four sections, to make the fullness easier to distribute.

Note: *Other floral designs from elsewhere in the book could be readily adapted for use with this pretty pillow.*

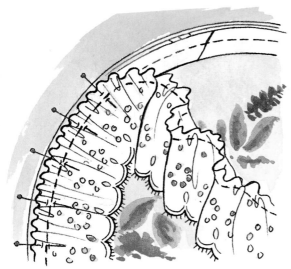

3 With the right sides of the fabric together, pin the frill to the embroidered and piped circle. Gather the frill by pulling the gathering thread and distribute the fullness evenly. Match the line of the gathering thread to the line of the machine stitching on the piping. Tack (baste) in position.

Completing the cover:
1 Place the embroidered section face down onto the right side of the cushion back, making sure that the frill is hidden inside. Pin the edges together along the line of tacking (basting). Ensure that the zip is half open so that the cover can be turned right side out after stitching.
2 Tack (baste) and machine stitch along the previous stitching lines.
3 Remove the tacking (basting) and gathering threads, trim the turnings and clip the curves.
4 Turn right sides out and press lightly, but avoid pressing the frill.

Making the pad:
1 Use the tracing paper circle again to cut two circles from plain cotton.
2 Place right sides together, pin and machine stitch a 1.5 cm (⅝ in) seam, leaving a 10 cm (4 in) opening.
3 Trim and clip the turnings, turn right sides out and press.
4 Insert the filling, adding spoonfuls of your chosen herb or pot pourri mixture as you go.
5 Pin the folded edges of the opening together, and machine stitch.
6 Place pad inside the cover and close zip.

Berlin woolwork set
Berlin woolwork was one of the most popular forms of canvaswork during the 19th century. It was so named because, at the beginning of that century, hand-painted paper charts were first printed in the city and these became widely available for use by women embroidering decorative pieces for their homes. The fashion for this type of embroidery quickly spread throughout Europe and even as far as America. The charts were in themselves, works of art, depicting domestic animals, hunting scenes and, most popular of all, luxuriant bunches and garlands of mixed flowers. The stitch most used to work these embroideries was cross stitch, which gave a very hard-wearing fabric suitable for chair seats, foot stools and other soft furnishings.

The design for this curtain tie-back and fingerplate set is taken from an original 19th century chart. To reduce bulk, the fingerplate design is adapted to be worked on evenweave fabric with stranded cotton.

Curtain tie-back:
REQUIREMENTS
For one tie-back:
White interlock canvas (Zweigart E604A) mesh size 10, a piece 72 cm x 32 cm (28 in x 12½ in)
DMC tapestry wools – colours and quantities as indicated on the chart
Tapestry needle size 20
Metric pattern guide paper
Pencil and water-soluble pen
Embroidery frame
Squared tracing paper
Coloured pencils
Black velvet furnishing fabric the same size as canvas
Dressmaker's pins
Tacking (basting) thread
Needle for sewing
Black thread for machine sewing
1.75 m (62 in) green cord
2 brass D rings and 1 brass hook
*(See **Getting started** page 15 for mounting canvas in a frame and stretching worked canvas, page 16 for reversing a chart, page 21 for clipping curves, and page 19 for slip stitch)*

These traditional Berlin work designs have a depth and richness of colour that creates a feeling of elegant living that is timeless.

1 Draw up the shape of the tie-back on pattern guide paper, and cut out. Place the pattern on the canvas and draw round it with a water-soluble pen, taking care that the lower straight edge is parallel to the canvas threads. Draw the centre line as a guide to placing the design.
2 Mount the canvas in the frame.
3 Start stitching the design, placing the tip of the extreme left-hand leaf five canvas threads from the centre line and 5.5 cm (2¼ in) down from the top edge. Stitch each cross over one intersection of the canvas threads.
4 When the design has been completed, reverse the chart and repeat for the back of the tie-back, this time placing the tip of the extreme right-hand leaf five canvas threads from the centre line and on the same thread counted from the top edge.
5 Fill in the background to cover the drawn pattern shape.
6 Remove the work from the frame and stretch the canvas.

Making up the tie-back:
1 Cut away excess canvas, leaving 1.5 cm (⅝ in) turnings. Place the work face down on the right side of the velvet and cut out the backing using the canvas as a guide.
2 With right sides together, pin, tack (baste) and machine stitch just inside the edge of the embroidery, leaving a 15 cm (6 in) opening along the lower edge.

> **Note:** If you prefer, you could work the floral design on the front of the tie-back, and fill-in the return half with the dark colour. To make a pair of tie-backs that have the floral design on one side only, reverse the design to make a mirror-image, and follow the instructions for completing the tie-back.

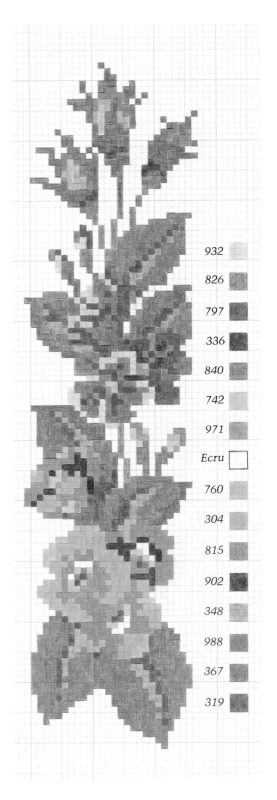

932
826
797
336
840
742
971
Ecru
760
304
815
902
348
988
367
319

3 Trim turnings and clip curves. Turn right sides out and slip stitch the opening closed.
4 Press the tie-back under a damp cloth and gently ease it to shape.
5 Slip stitch the cord round the edge, and attach a D ring at each end on the back of the tie-back.
6 Fix the brass hook to the wall beside the window, and hang up the tie-back.

Fingerplate:

REQUIREMENTS
14 count Aida evenweave fabric (Zweigart E3706) in black – approximately 34 x 34 cm (13¼ x 13¼ in) square
Tapestry needle size 26
DMC stranded cottons – one skein of each colour as indicated on the chart
Embroidery hoop
Clear plastic fingerplate with a recess (these are widely available in specialist handicraft and needlecraft shops)
50 cm (½ yd) Vilene 'Wundaweb' (or similar soft, hem-bonding strip)
Small piece of thin card
*(See **Getting started** page 21 for how to mitre corners)*

To work the embroidery:
1 Mount the fabric in the hoop.
2 Follow the chart and use two strands of thread throughout. Stitch each cross over one thread block. Remember – it is essential to work in a good light when stitching on a dark fabric.
3 When the design is completed, remove the fabric from the hoop. Press lightly on the wrong side with the work face down on a clean soft towel.

Making up the fingerplate:
1 Measure the recess in the plastic fingerplate and cut a template from thin card to fit comfortably, but not too tightly.
2 Trim excess fabric leaving 5 cm (2 in) all round the embroidery.
3 Place the template in position on the back of the embroidery. Fold and press the fabric over the card.
4 Remove the template, and trim the turnings to 1.5 cm (⅝ in). Mitre the corners.
5 Secure the turnings with hem-bonding strip, as manufacturer's instructions.
6 Place the work in the plastic fingerplate and fix above the door handle.

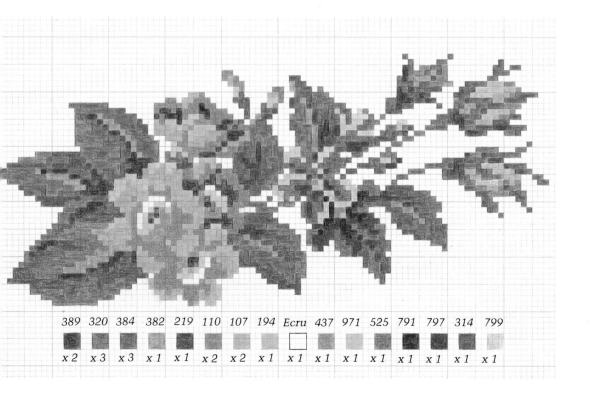

389	320	384	382	219	110	107	194	Ecru	437	971	525	791	797	314	799
x 2	x 3	x 3	x 1	x 1	x 2	x 2	x 1	x 1	x 1	x 1	x 1	x 1	x 1	x 1	x 1

Picture mounts

Most people have a special photograph or precious print which would be enhanced by being displayed in a unique frame.

Here are two mounts which are designed to be framed behind glass. The oval mount is decorated with sprays of flowers around a gold-edged window. The design for the rectangular mount uses a pattern which is thought to have originated in Greece.

Oval picture mount:

REQUIREMENTS

Linda evenweave fabric (Zweigart E1235) in Ivory (colour number 264) approximately 28 cm (11 in) square
Tapestry needle size 26
DMC stranded cotton – one skein of each colour as indicated on the chart
Embroidery hoop
15.5 cm (6 in) square picture frame
Cream mounting board approximately 18 cm (7 in) square
Craft knife
Ruler and pencil
Tracing paper
All-purpose adhesive
Masking tape.
*(See **Getting started** page 21 for how to mitre corners)*

Stitching the embroidery:

1 Mount the fabric in the hoop, positioning it so that the design will fall in the centre.
2 Stitch the design using two strands of thread and forming each cross over two threads of fabric in each direction.

3 When the embroidery is complete, remove it from the hoop and press lightly on the wrong side with the work face down on a clean soft towel.

Making up the picture mount:
1 With a sharp craft knife cut the mounting board to fit inside the picture frame comfortably, allowing a little space all round to accommodate the fabric.
2 Place a piece of tracing paper over the embroidery, and carefully trace an oval 3 mm (⅛ in) inside the cross-stitched oval.
3 Place the tracing on the mounting board so that the oval is 4 cm (1⅝ in) from the top, base and right-hand edges. Secure in position with masking tape.

The decorative cross stitch picture mounts on these pages show how versatile the effects can be. The 19th century album-style mount evokes a wistfulness for days-gone-by, while the classic scroll design has a robust, traditional appeal, that suites its polished wood frame.

4 Prick through tracing paper with a pin at small intervals all round the oval. Remove the tracing paper and join up the pin-pricks with a pencil.
5 With a sharp knife, carefully cut out the oval window.

6 Cut out the centre of the cross-stitched oval 2 cm (¾ in) inside the stitching. Clip the curves to 6 mm (¼ in) from the edge of the stitching.

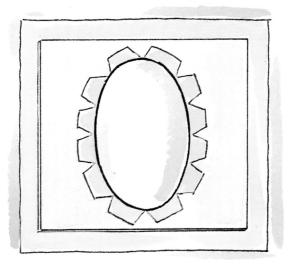

7 Put the embroidery face down on a clean surface and place the board window over the embroidered frame. Spread a thin layer of adhesive all round the oval edge of the board. Turn-in the clipped fabric and stick down firmly. Check that the position is correct and adjust if necessary before the adhesive dries.

8 Trim away the excess fabric to leave 4 cm (1⅝ in) turnings all round the board. Stick the turnings to the back of the board, mitring the corners as you go.
9 Position your favourite photograph behind the embroidered window and secure it in place with pieces of masking tape. Put the mount in the frame and assemble the back of the frame.

Rectangular picture mount:
REQUIREMENTS
*Dublin 22-count linen fabric (Zweigart
   E3604) in 'Raw linen' (Colour 53)
   approximately 36 x 40 cm (14 x 16 in)
Tapestry needle size 26
DMC stranded cotton – one skein of each
   colour as indicated on the chart
Embroidery hoop
Picture frame 19 x 23 cm (7½ x 9in)
Brown mounting board approximately
   21 x 26 cm (8 x 10 in)
Craft knife
Ruler and pencil
All-purpose adhesive
Masking tape*

Stitching the embroidery:
1 Mount the fabric in the hoop, and stitch the design following the chart. Turn the chart round to complete the other half of the design. Dublin linen has a loose weave, so take care not to pull the stitches too tight, as this will make holes in the fabric. Use two strands of thread and stitch each cross over two threads in each direction.
2 When the embroidery is complete, remove it from the frame and press lightly on the wrong side with the work face down on a clean soft towel.

Making up the picture mount:
1 Cut a piece of mounting board to fit inside the frame comfortably, allowing a little space all round.
2 Measure a rectangle 3 mm (⅛ in) smaller on each side than the cross-stitched rectangle. Draw a window this size in the centre of the board. Cut it out with a sharp craft knife.
3 Cut the centre of the fabric away leaving 2 cm (¾ in) turnings inside the embroidered rectangle. Clip into the corners diagonally.
4 Complete as for the oval mount, taking care that the threads of the fabric are in line with the straight edges of the board.

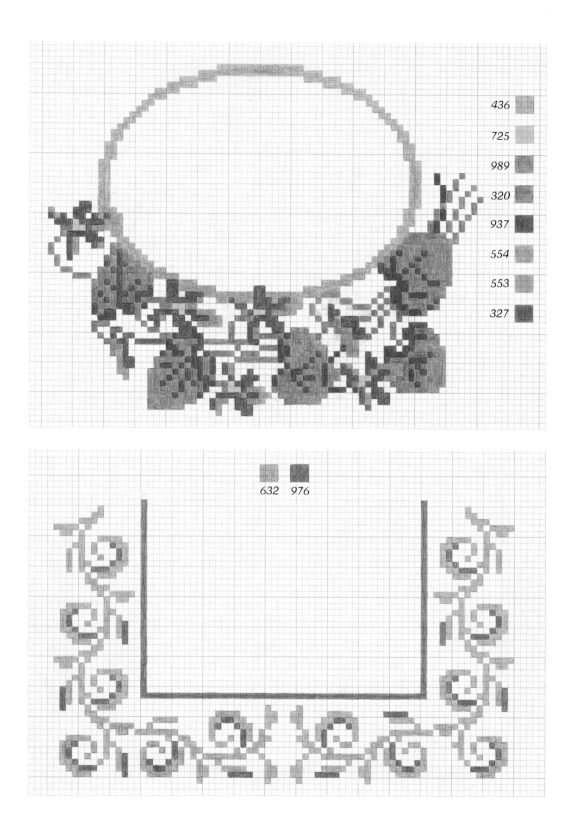

436
725
989
320
937
554
553
327

632   976

Chapter 4
Traditional gifts

A traditional sampler

The earliest samplers served as a record of stitches and patterns and so they would include a variety of different stitches. This 'reference library' could then be drawn on by the needlewoman when making items for the home or articles of clothing.

Later, in the 18th and 19th centuries, samplers became the means by which a young girl could learn and practice the needlework skills she would require as a housewife. These samplers, mostly executed in cross stitch, are a delight. They nearly always incorporate the name of the young needlewoman and the date. I love to speculate on the child who worked the sampler, her life and her times and wonder if the child enjoyed her task or if she found it an irksome chore. The fact that sometimes there are mistakes makes them all the more charming and individual.

These schoolgirl samplers often contain alphabets in different type faces, some plain and some highly decorative, as well as numbers, all surrounded by borders. Sometimes some personal detail of the child's life would be recorded – a favourite pet for example, or often a worthy and uplifting sentiment would be included.

I have designed a sampler here which incorporates alphabets, numbers and borders and, while it is attractive just as it is, I have also tried to show in the three projects that follow the traditional sampler, that the different elements can be used to create your own unique pieces of work.

REQUIREMENTS
Linda evenweave fabric (Zweigart E1235) in
    Ivory (colour 264) 50 x 56 cm (20 x 22 in)
Tapestry needle size 26
DMC stranded cottons – one skein of each
    colour as indicated on the chart
Tacking (basting) thread and needle
Embroidery hoop
Cream mounting board 50 x 56 cm
    (20 x 22 in)
Craft knife
Buttonhole thread for lacing
Large sewing needle
*(See **Getting started** page 23 for how to lace*
embroidery over card)

Stitching the embroidery:
1 Run a row of tacking (basting) stitches across the width of the fabric about 9 cm

(3½ in) from the top edge. This line marks the top of the first row of rosebud letters.
2 Place the fabric in the embroidery hoop and work this row of letters first. Use two strands of thread throughout and stitch each cross over two fabric threads in each direction.
3 Follow the chart and complete the embroidery. (You may find it easiest to work the two long side borders last of all.)
4 Remove the work from the hoop and place it face down on a soft clean towel. Press lightly on the wrong side.

Mounting and framing the sampler:
1 Withdraw a thread of fabric 6 cm (2⅜ in) all round from the edge of the embroidery. Cut away excess fabric along this line.
2 Measure 3 cm (1¼ in) all round from the edge of the embroidery, and use a craft knife to cut the mounting board to this size.
3 Lace the embroidery firmly over the board, using the buttonhole thread. Make sure that the edges of the board are parallel to the threads of the fabric.
4 Have your sampler framed, using a frame moulding in a style and colour that does not dominate the embroidery.

Three ways to use the sampler library:
There are many gifts which could make use of the letters, numbers and borders from the sampler. Here are just three simple ideas to show the varied ways of applying the different elements.

> **Note:** *It is well worth protecting a piece of embroidery from dust by mounting it in a frame. It is preferable to use non-reflective glass as this does not obscure the stitching as much as plain glass.*

A guest towel

This sampler variation uses the leafy border applied to a small hand towel, but gives it a different feel by using different shades of green, and by edging it top and bottom with a border of pretty little rosebuds taken from the first alphabet.

REQUIREMENTS
A small hand towel with an evenweave
    band (these are available at specialist
    needlecraft shops and suppliers)

Small embroidery hoop
Tapestry needle size 26
DMC stranded cottons – one skein of each
   chosen colour
Tacking (basting) thread and needle

Stitching the embroidery:
1 Find the centre of the evenweave band on
the towel and mark it with a tacking
(basting) thread. Place the design so that
there are the same number of threads above
and below it on the band.
2 Starting with the centre of the chart on
the centre of the towel, work outwards,
using two strands of thread and stitching
each cross over one block of threads.

*Besides being an attractive piece of work in its
own right, this traditional sampler can be used as
a design reference for future projects.*

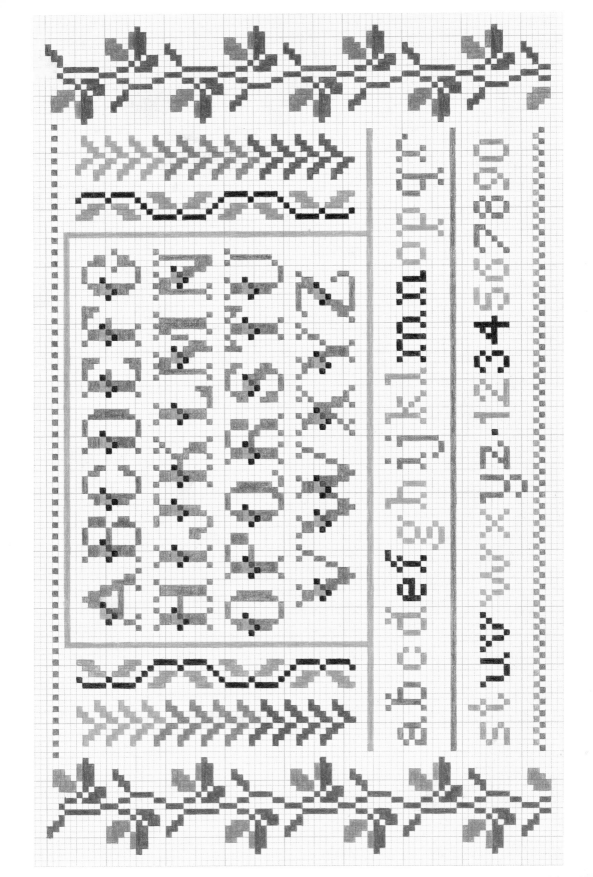

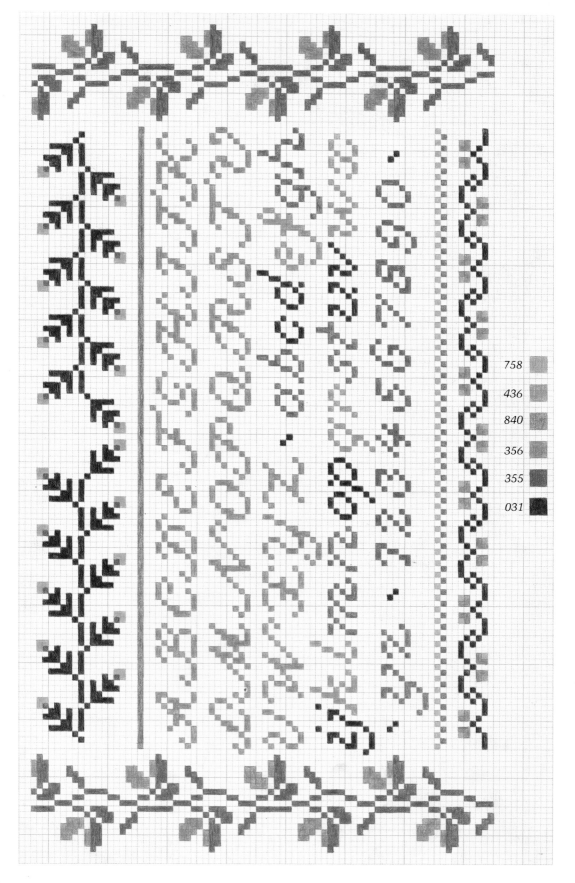

758

436

840

356

355

031

Finishing the towel:

1 Remove the work from the hoop. Press the embroidery lightly on the wrong side, with the work face down on a clean soft towel.

2 Gently steam the towelling to lift the pile if it has been flattened by the hoop.

An initialled pocket

This project uses bright colours to personalize a child's tee shirt. The pretend pocket shows initials using the letters of the first alphabet on the sampler but omitting the rosebuds. You could, of course, incorporate these into a design to make a pocket with a distinctly feminine touch.

REQUIREMENTS
A plain-coloured tee shirt
12-count squared tracing paper
Coloured pencil
12 mesh waste canvas 27 cm (10½ in)
    square
Tacking (basting) thread and needle
Crewel embroidery needle size 7
Small embroidery hoop
Water soluble pen
DMC stranded cottons – one skein of each
    chosen colour
*(See **Getting started** page 16 for using squared tracing paper to adapt a chart, and page 18 for using waste canvas)*

Note: *If you cannot find a hand towel with an evenweave band already in place, use a plain hand towel. Stitch the embroidery on a piece of 14-count Aida fabric, marked by a tacking (basting) thread to the width and depth of the finished band. When the embroidery is complete, cut out the band leaving 1.5 cm (⅝ in) turnings. Press-in the raw edges pin and slipstitch in place.*

Adapting the chart:

The initials use the capital letters of the first alphabet on the large sampler (see chart page 60) but omit the rosebud motif. Using the squared tracing paper and coloured pencil, adapt the chart to fit your chosen initials. (It may be necessary to move the border pattern on each side apart slightly to accommodate any wider letters.)

Stitching the embroidery:

1 Decide where you want the 'pocket' and tack (baste) the waste canvas in position. This will be easy to do if you put a piece of stiff card inside the tee shirt to prevent stitching the back and front together. Make sure that the tee shirt lies flat but not stretched under the canvas.

2 Mark the position of the 'pocket' with the water soluble pen.

Personalized designs like this colourful initialled pocket are popular with all ages. By choosing a few patterns from the sampler library, and selecting embroidery threads to complement the background fabric, you can create unique designs which are sure to be appreciated.

3 Mount in the embroidery hoop. The piece of canvas is large enough to project beyond the hoop. (The tee shirt fabric would be too stretchy to put in the hoop on its own.)
4 Follow your adapted chart, inserting the correct initials. Use three strands of thread in the crewel needle, and stitch each cross over one intersection of canvas threads.

Finishing the tee shirt:
Remove the waste canvas. Allow the tee shirt to dry slightly, then press it lightly on the wrong side with the embroidery face down on a clean soft towel.

Wedding anniversary sampler
This simple chart commemorates a wedding anniversary and can easily be adapted to fit any names and dates. 'Special occasion' samplers have become very popular and are a pleasure to give as well as to receive. There are many landmarks in our lives that are worthy of celebration in this way.

REQUIREMENTS
Linda evenweave fabric (Zweigart E1235) in White approximately 25 x 25 cm (10 x 10 in) square
Tapestry needle size 26
Embroidery hoop
DMC stranded cottons – one skein of each chosen colour

14-count squared tracing paper
Coloured pencils
Thick card and strong thread for lacing the finished embroidery
Mounting board
Picture frame
*(See **Getting started** page 16 for adapting a chart on squared tracing paper, and page 23 for how to lace embroidery over card)*

Adapting the chart:
1 Draw the appropriate names onto the squared tracing paper, centring them one above the other, and with the correct number of squares between. Draw the date and position that in the same way.
2 The size of the pink box surrounding the names may have to be changed and the side patterns moved further apart. Adjust these on the squared tracing paper if necessary.
3 When you are satisfied with your new chart, you can begin to stitch.

Stitching the embroidery:
1 Mount the fabric in the hoop and following your chart, stitch using two strands of thread, forming each cross over two fabric threads in each direction.
2 When the stitching is finished, remove the fabric from the hoop and press lightly on the wrong side, with the work face down on a soft towel.

This wedding anniversary sampler would make a thoughtful gift as a reminder of a special day. You could select the thread and mount colours to suit the decor.

Mounting and framing your work:
1 Choose a ready-made frame to suit the piece of work. Cut a piece of thick card to the correct size and lace the embroidery over it with strong thread.
2 Choose a piece of coloured mounting board and have a framer cut the mount to the correct size with an oval window.
3 Assemble the mount and embroidery in the frame with the backing.

Variations:
Have fun designing your own sampler for a special occasion by using other elements from the main sampler chart. Try different fabrics and colours of thread; make your samplers small and simple or large and complicated; try designing a sampler to include a favourite quotation or saying – the possibilities are endless.

There are also lots of other gift ideas to make using the main chart. The border patterns could be used on tray cloths, table cloths or napkins, or perhaps on a dressing table runner and the alphabets can be used for all kinds of personal belongings.

Embroidered greetings cards

Attractive greetings cards are expensive to buy and invariably end up in the waste paper bin. A hand-embroidered card, however, would be unlikely to meet the same fate, and would be more likely to be treasured for a long time, or even considered worthy of framing.

Here are two cards, one for Christmas and the other equally suitable for a birthday, Easter or Mother's Day. Both make use of ready-made presentation cards. These are constructed in three sections to take a piece of embroidery, so the back of your work will not be on display!

Primrose card

REQUIREMENTS

18 count Aida evenweave fabric (Zweigart E3793) in White approximately 20 x 20 cm (8 x 8 in) square
Small embroidery hoop
Tapestry needle size 26
DMC Flower threads – one skein of each colour as indicated on the chart
DMC large, cream presentation card design N2503
Masking tape
Double-sided adhesive tape

Working the embroidery:

1 Place the fabric in the embroidery hoop and, following the chart and using a single strand of thread, stitch the primroses. Work each cross over a single block of threads.
2 Remove the work from the hoop and press it lightly on the wrong side with the stitching face down on a soft clean towel.

Making up the card:

1 Position the window of the card over the embroidery. Turn the card over and cut away the excess fabric leaving an extra 2 cm (¾ in) all round.
2 Fix the embroidery in position behind the window with small pieces of masking tape placed at top and bottom.
3 Stick down the inside flap to cover the back of the embroidery using lengths of double-sided adhesive tape.

This primrose design captures all the freshness of the spring flowers. Not only is it perfect for a birthday and seasonal greetings card, but the design is adaptable enough to suit a variety of other uses. For example, you could change the background colour, or use the design to complement real primroses, by working the motif on a fabric câche pot, or you could add the primroses to table or bedlinen or use them for a box top or to decorate the corner of a slip-over book cover.

The Christmas card

REQUIREMENTS
14-count Damask Aida (Zweigart E3229) in
   White approximately 24 x 24 cm
   (9½ x 9½ in) square
Embroidery hoop
Tapestry needle size 26
DMC stranded cottons – one skein each,
   red 349 and green 702
One reel DMC light gold metallic thread
DMC large presentation card design N2505
   in Christmas red
Double-sided adhesive tape
Masking tape

Stitching the embroidery:

1 Place the fabric in the hoop. Follow the chart using two threads of stranded cotton and one of gold thread. Stitch each cross over one block of threads.

2 Remove the finished work from the hoop and press it lightly on the wrong side with the stitching face down on a clean soft towel. Make up the card in the same way as the primrose card.

> **Note:** *When using the metallic thread, use short lengths only, as the thread splits with use and tangles easily. Pull the stitches firmly as you sew.*

Variations:

Try making gift tags by stitching a single Christmas tree or holly sprig from the chart and cutting your own cards from coloured card. Punch a hole in the top left-hand corner of the finished tags and thread a length of cotton or glitter string through.

Decorate festive table linen with motifs, arranged in groups or individually. Another option is to embroider decorative bands on Christmas stockings.

This cheerful Christmas card design takes on a completely different appearance by changing the colour of the background, and the metallic threads really add a sparkle to the motifs.

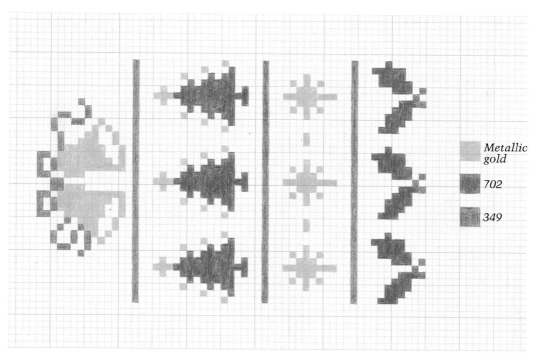

Metallic
gold

702

349

840

742

727

745

788

906

909

Gifts for a new baby

The arrival of a new baby is often the signal for a lot of energetic knitting and stitching. Many things can be passed on from one baby to the next, but it is nice to have some things that are uniquely special to a particular baby. The name Maria is used on this set of gifts, but any name can be substituted and the chart adjusted accordingly.

A Crib Quilt Cover

Finished quilt size is 56 x 68 cm
(22 x 26¾ in)
REQUIREMENTS
10-count squared tracing paper
Coloured pencils
60 cm (23½ in) white sheeting fabric
*   230 cm (90 in) wide*
10 mesh waste canvas 36 x 24 cm
*   (14 x 9½ in)*
Dark tacking (basting) thread and needle
Water-soluble pen
Crewel embroidery needle size 7
Large embroidery hoop
DMC stranded cottons – one skein of each
*   colour as indicated on the chart*
White thread for sewing machine
Dressmaker's pins
8 cm (3 in) white Velcro fastening strip

*(See **Getting started** page 16 for adapting a chart on squared tracing paper, page 17 for back stitch, and page 18 for how to use waste canvas)*

Adapting the chart:

1 On the squared tracing paper use coloured pencils to draw up the name of the baby, spacing the letters one square apart.
2 On another piece of tracing paper, work out the date using the upright numbers from the sampler chart on page 60. Leave three squares blank and position the date centrally below the name.
3 Draw the pink box around the name, and the pink hearts on each side of the date, adding more hearts if necessary.
4 Count 22 squares to the left of the box and mark this with a pencil. These squares will be occupied by the teddy bear.
5 Now find the centre of the design and mark this with a pencil.

A really special set like this is a wonderful, welcoming gift for a new baby.

Working the embroidery:

1 Tack the waste canvas 48 cm (19 in) up from the selvage on the sheeting fabric, making sure that it is in the centre.
2 Mount the fabric in the embroidery hoop.
3 Following the printed chart, stitch the butterfly and boat borders first, centring them in the width of the fabric. The bottom edge of the embroidery should be 50 cm (19½ in) up from the selvage. Use three strands of thread throughout and work each cross over one intersection of canvas threads.
4 When the long borders are complete, use your adapted chart to stitch the rest of the design. Make sure that the centre of the chart corresponds with the centre of the borders.
5 When all the cross stitch is complete, remove the waste canvas. Allow the fabric to dry slightly, then press the work on the wrong side, face down on a clean soft towel.
6 Put the work back in the hoop and work the mouth of the teddy bear in back stitch.

Making the quilt cover:

1 On the wrong side of the fabric, use a water-soluble pen to draw dots to lightly mark a line below the embroidery, 18 cm (7 in) from the bottom row of stitching. Fold along this line with right sides out. Press well.

2 In the same way, mark a line 50 cm (19⅝ in) above the bottom row of stitching. With right sides out, fold along line; press.
3 Mark the side seams 56 cm (22 in) apart with the water soluble pen, making sure that the design is in the centre of the cover.

4 Machine stitch a double hem on the back of the cover, 68 cm (26¾ in) from the top fold line.

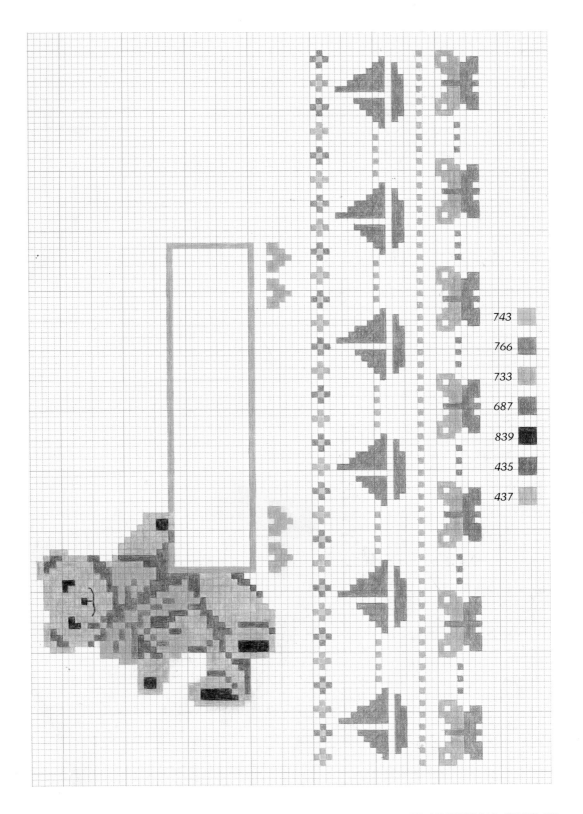

743
766
733
687
839
435
437

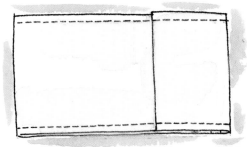

5 With wrong sides out, fold the cover with the large flap outside. Pin and machine stitch the side seams.
6 Trim the turnings. Turn the flap and then the whole cover right sides out and press, avoiding the embroidery (which should always be pressed from the wrong side).
7 Remove any pen marks with the corner of a clean, damp cloth.
8 Cut the Velcro strip into four and stitch at equal intervals along the opening.

A pretty towelling bib

REQUIREMENTS
A ready-made towelling bib with an
evenweave band – these are widely
available at specialist needlecraft shops
Small embroidery hoop
Tapestry needle size 26
DMC stranded cottons – one skein of each
colour as indicated on the chart
Squared tracing paper
Coloured pencils

Adapting the chart:
1 On the squared tracing paper, draw the baby's name, spacing the letters so that they are one square apart.
2 Count the number of thread blocks that there are across the bib and centre the name in the same number of squares on the tracing paper.
3 Colour-in the right number of hearts each side of the name to fill the remaining space.

Stitching the embroidery:
1 Mark the centre of the evenweave band with a pin. Make sure that the centre of your adapted chart is on the centre of the band and that the design is positioned to leave the same number of thread blocks above and below it.
2 Using an embroidery hoop stitch the design using two strands of thread. Work each cross over one thread block.

3 When the embroidery is finished, remove the bib from the hoop and press it lightly on the wrong side, with the work face down on a clean towel. If the towelling has been crushed by the hoop, steam it lightly.

A laundry bag
50 cm (½ yd) White Oslo evenweave fabric
(Zweigart E3947)
50 cm (½ yd) white sheeting fabric
Tapestry needle size 26
Large embroidery hoop
DMC stranded cottons – one skein of each
colour as indicated on the chart
Water-soluble pen
Coat-hanger
Dressmaker's pins
White thread for sewing machine.
1 m (1 yd) white satin bias binding.
50 cm (½ yd) white double satin ribbon
4 cm (⅛ in) white Velcro fastening strip
*(See **Getting started** page 20 for binding a*
raw edge)

Cutting out the laundry bag:
1 Cut a piece of Oslo 50 x 35 cm (19⅝ x 13¾ in).
2 Cut a second piece of Oslo 50 x 108 cm (19⅝ x 42½ in).
3 Cut two pieces of sheeting to these same sizes for the bag lining.

Stitching the embroidery:
(See instructions for the quilt cover for how to adapt the chart.)
1 Use two strands of thread and work each cross over two threads in each direction.
2 On the smaller piece of Oslo, work the main design 10 cm (4 in) up from one long edge. Make sure the design is centred in the fabric width.
3 On the large piece of Oslo, embroider the border patterns 32 cm (12½ in) down from the top edge. Make sure the border is centred on the fabric.
4 When the embroidery is complete, press it on the wrong side with the work face down on a clean soft towel.

> **Note:** *Although white is a traditional colour for baby items, you could also work the designs on pastel towelling. Deep dyes would also be attractive, with the embroidery colours deepened accordingly.*

Making up the laundry bag:

1 Place the coat-hanger centrally on the smaller piece of Oslo, approximately 18 cm (7 in) above the lower edge of the embroidery. With a water-soluble pen, lightly draw dots at intervals to mark the shape of the hanger. This will be the seam line. Trim the lower edge of the fabric 6 cm (2¼ in) below the bottom of the embroidery.

2 Fold the large piece of Oslo with the embroidery to the front and 9 cm (3½ in) up from the fold. Trim the fabric to 40 cm (15¾ in) from the fold.

3 Place the large and small pieces together with top edges matching. Cut away excess fabric to leave 1.5 cm (⅝ in) turnings at the seam line.

4 With right sides together, machine stitch the seam leaving 1 cm (⅜ in) open in the centre for the hook of the hanger to pass through. Trim the turnings and press the seam open.
5 Measure the width of the hanger and cut away excess fabric at the sides, leaving 1.5 cm (⅝in) extra for seam allowance.
6 Make up the lining in the same way.
7 With wrong sides together, match the seams of lining and bag and pin together.

8 Making sure that the two layers of fabric lie flat with edges matching, bind the two shorter edges with satin bias binding.

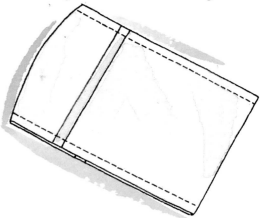

9 With the embroidery inside, stitch the side seams, with the flap tucked inside.
10 Trim the turnings and turn the embroidered side out. Press seams lightly.
11 Remove any pen marks with the corner of a clean damp cloth.
12 Cut the Velcro in half and stitch the pieces under the flap.
13 Insert the coat-hanger through the gap in the top seam and trim with a ribbon bow.

Chapter 5
Small gifts

Pin cushion and needlecase set

Inspired by the richly coloured, exotic embroideries of India, this decorative set, based on simple geometric patterns is simple enough for a beginner. In days gone by articles such as these were made to practice sewing skills and were among the first to be made by a young girl.

The pincushion

REQUIREMENTS
*14 count Aida evenweave fabric (Zweigart
    3706 colour 13) 25 x 25 cm
    (10 x 10 in square)
DMC stranded cotton in the colours
    indicated on the chart
Red velvet 18 x 18 m (7 x 7 in) square
Polyester toy filling
75 cm (⅞ yd) dark red cord
DMC perle cotton 815
Small embroidery hoop
Tapestry needle size 26
Red sewing machine thread
Tacking (basting) thread
Sewing needle and pins
(See **Getting started** page 19 for slip stitch,
and page 21 for clipping corners)*

Stitching the embroidery:

1 Place the Aida fabric in the embroidery hoop. Using two strands of thread throughout, and working each cross over one block of threads, stitch the design following the chart.
2 Remove the fabric from the hoop. Place the work right side down onto a clean soft towel and press lightly with an iron.
3 Trim the fabric to 2 cm (¾ in) from the edge of the embroidery, leaving the same number of thread blocks on each side.

Making up the pin cushion:

1 Cut a piece of velvet to the same size as the trimmed embroidered fabric. With the right sides of the fabric together, pin, tack and machine stitch the velvet to the embroidered fabric. Stitch 1 cm (⅜ in) from the edge of the embroidery, making sure there are an equal number of threads on each side. Leave an opening of 6 cm (2½ in).

Rich colours make this tassel-trimmed pin cushion and needlecase look rather special. You could make the set even more exotic by adding perfume oil to the filling.

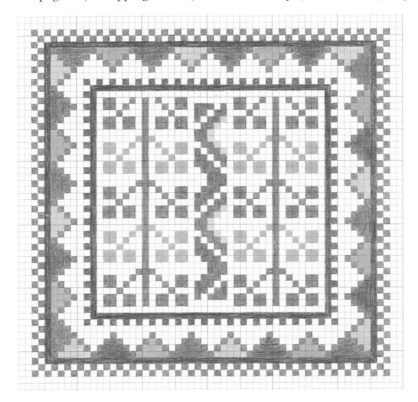

One skein of each colour is sufficient to embroider the needlecase and pin cushion. Check with the key on page 81.

2 Remove the tacking (basting) threads and trim the turnings to 6 mm (¼ in). Clip the corners and turn the cushion right sides out. Gently push the corners to shape with a knitting needle or other blunt tip.

3 Pad the cushion firmly with toy filling, easing the filling well into the corners, and slip stitch the opening closed.

Trimming the pin cushion:

1 Starting at a corner, slip stitch the cord in place over the seam, making a small loop at each corner. To make a loop, secure the cord end with a few stitches at one corner, and twist the cord over itself. Secure the loop with a stitch through all thicknesses. Continue by slip stitching the cord round the cushion, making equal sized loops as you go. Hide the cord ends at the back of the last loop and oversew neatly to secure.

2 Make four tassels from perlé cotton and stitch one to a cord loop at each corner of the pin cushion.

Making tassels:

These little trims are extremely easy to make and they add a luxurious and rather sophisticated finishing touch to a design.

1 To make a tassel about 5 cm (2 in) long, cut a piece of stiff card into a 10 x 5 cm (4 x 2 in) rectangle. Wind the thread round and round the card, keeping the thread straight and taut. Decide how plump you wish the tassel to be, then cut through the threads at the lower edge of the card.

2 Using a length of the same thread, tie the threads together through the middle. Do not trim the ends of the tie threads yet.

3 Wind another length of thread round the threads to shape the tassel, secure with a knot, then pass these thread ends into the centre of the tassel to neaten. Trim the lower edge of the tassel to the required length. Use the thread at the top of the tassel and a sewing needle to stitch the tassel into place.

> **Note:** *You could make the pin cushion more exotic by adding a few drops of perfume oil such as sandalwood or musk to the polyester filling, or by adding some fragrant pot pourri.*

The needlecase

REQUIREMENTS

14 count Aida evenweave fabric (Zweigart 3706 colour 13), a piece measuring 35 x 25 cm (14 x 10 in)
DMC stranded cotton in the colours indicated on the chart
Tapestry needle size 26
Small embroidery hoop
Thin card
Ruler and pencil
Craft knife
All purpose clear adhesive
Red satin 24 x 16 cm (9½ x 6½ in)
Soft iron-on interfacing 24 x 16 cm (9½ x 6½ in)
Paper-backed, double-sided, fusible interfacing (Bondaweb) 22 x 14 cm (8½ x 5½ in)
Red felt 21 cm (8 in) square
50 cm (½ yd) dark red cord
DMC perlé cotton 815 to make tassels (one skein is sufficient to make six small tassels)
Machine sewing thread
Sewing needle
Pinking shears (optional)
*(See **Getting started** page 21 for how to mitre corners)*

Stitching the embroidery:

1 Place the fabric in the embroidery hoop, positioning it so that the embroidery will be centred in the right-hand half of the fabric.
2 Using two strands of thread throughout, and working each cross over one block of evenweave threads, stitch the design following the chart.
3 Remove the fabric from the hoop. Place the work right side down onto a clean soft towel and press lightly with an iron.

Assembling the cover:

1 Trim the fabric so that ten thread blocks remain outside the stitching on the right-hand side, and on the top and lower edge. Trim the fabric 11.5 cm (4⅝ in) from the left-hand side of the stitching.

2 Cut two pieces of card 11.5 x 9.5 cm (4½ x 3¾ in). Place the cards on the wrong side of the embroidered fabric, five thread blocks in from each edge, leaving three thread blocks in the centre to make the fold.

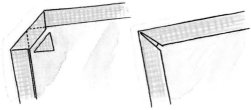

3 Apply a small amount of adhesive all round the edge of the fabric, then turn-in the edges to stick to the card. Fold and stick the corners into neat mitres as you go.

| 309 | 433 | 562 | 725 | 354 | 799 |

Making the lining and the pages:

1 Iron the interfacing to the wrong side of the red satin lining fabric. Cut out a 22 x 14 cm (8¾ x 5½ in) rectangle from this.
2 Fold a single 1.5 cm (⅝ in) turning to wrong side of fabric, and mitre the corners. Press. Secure corners with adhesive.
3 Cut a piece of Bondaweb the same size as the finished satin lining and, following manufacturers instructions, iron it onto the wrong side of the satin. Remove the protective paper from the back of the Bondaweb, and iron the lining, sticky side down, onto the back of the cover.
4 Cut the felt square in half, using pinking shears, and trim the other long edges to match. Trim 2 cm (¾ in) from each short edge, to make two pages 17 x 10 cm (6¾ x 4 in). Place the pages together and, matching the centres of the pages to the inside centre of the cover, stitch through all layers.

Trimming the needlecase:

Knot the length of cord round the fold of the needlecase. Knot each end 7 cm (2¾ in) from the lower edge, and trim each end with a tassel made from perlé cotton.

Jewellery roll and lipstick case

A few years ago I was given a jewellery roll and soon discovered that, although I have no priceless gems to take on holiday with me, even my few, but much-loved trinkets travel better in a specially made case than in the plastic bags I used before.

Even though this project may appear rather complicated, only basic sewing skills are needed in the construction and the matching lipstick case is easy to make. By enlarging this slightly you could also make a holder for a perfume bottle.

Jewellery roll

REQUIREMENTS

Linda evenweave fabric (Zweigart 1235) in
  Ivory (colour 264) approximately
  42 x 34 cm (16½ in x 13½ in)
DMC stranded cottons in the colours
  indicated on the chart (one skein of each
  colour is enough for both projects)
Tapestry needle size 26
Large embroidery hoop
70 gm (2½ oz) polyester wadding
  approximately 35 x 27 cm (13¾ x 10½ in)
Small amount of polyester toy filling
One snap fastener
50 cm (½ yd) ivory brushed satin for the
  lining
18 cm (7 in) ivory zip fastener
Ivory thread for sewing machine
Sewing needle
Dressmaking pins
Tacking (basting) thread
1 m (1 yd) narrow pink double satin ribbon
*(See **Getting started** page 17 for French*
knots, and page 22 for inserting a zip, page
21 for clipping corners and page 19 for top
stitching)

Stitching the embroidery:

1 Place the evenweave fabric in the embroidery hoop so that the finished spray of roses will be in the centre of the fabric.
2 Work the cross stitch following the chart and using two strands of thread throughout. Stitch each cross over two fabric threads in each direction.
3 When the cross stitch is complete, use one strand of brown thread number 975 to work a few French knots in the centre of each flower.
4 Remove the finished embroidery from the hoop and press it lightly on the wrong side, work face down on a clean towel.

Making up the embroidery roll:

1 With the embroidery positioned in the centre of the long edge, cut the embroidered piece to make a rectangle 31 cm x 23 cm (12¼ in x 9 in). Pull out fabric threads at these measurements as a cutting guide.
2 Cut a piece of the lining the same size.
3 Cut the wadding to the same size.

Making the pocket section:

1 Cut a second piece of lining fabric 30 cm x 23 cm (11¾ in x 9 in).

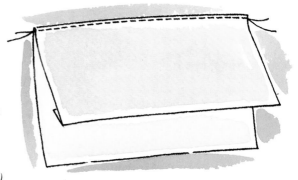

2 With the right side of the fabric outside, make a fold 19 cm (7½ in) from one short edge. Press and machine stitch along the fold close to the edge. Make a second fold 1.5 cm (⅝ in) from the other short edge, and press.
3 Cut a third piece of lining fabric 20 cm x 23 cm (8 in x 9 in). Fold it in half with right side outside to make a piece 10 cm x 23 cm (4 in x 9 in). Press to shape.
4 Insert the zip between these two folded edges.

Making the ring holder:

1 Cut a strip of lining fabric 20 cm x 7 cm (8 in x 2¾ in).
2 Place the long edges together with right side inside. Pin, tack (baste) and machine stitch a 1 cm (⅜ in) seam down the long edge and across one end.
3 Trim the turnings to 6 mm (¼ in) and turn right side out.
4 Fix the head of the snap fastener to the closed end of the ring holder, following the manufacturer's instructions.
5 Fill the tube firmly with toy filling and tack (baste) in place, 2 cm (¾ in) below zip.
6 Fix the base of the snap fastener into place on the pocket, positioning it to correspond with the head.

Assembling the jewellery roll:

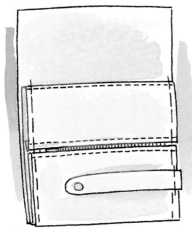 

1 Tack (baste) the pocket assembly to the right side of the lining piece, matching the lower edges together.

This set would make a lovely gift for a new bride, or for someone who travels often.

2 Place the embroidered piece and the pocket section together with right sides facing, and place both on the piece of wadding. Pin, tack (baste) and machine stitch a 1.5 cm (⅝ in) seam all round, leaving a 10 cm (4 in) opening at the top.

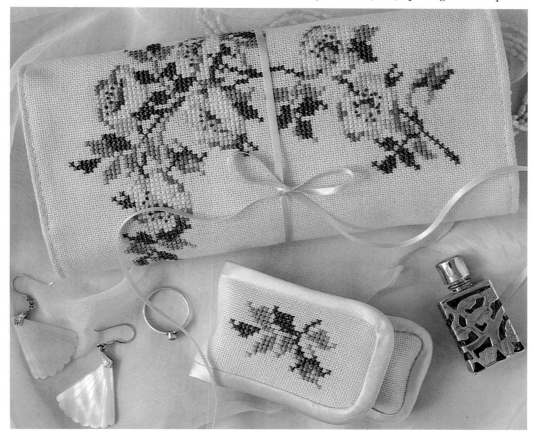

3 Remove the tacking (basting) thread. Trim the wadding as close to the stitching as possible and trim the turnings to 6 mm (¼ in). Clip the corners. Turn right sides out, gently push out the corners with a knitting needle, and press lightly under a clean cloth.
4 Cut the ribbon into a 86 cm (34 in) length. Fold it in half and insert it into the centre of the opening, and tack (baste) it into place.
5 With the sewing machine set on a fairly large stitch, top stitch all round close to the edge, catching-in the ribbon.

The lipstick case

REQUIREMENTS
Linda evenweave fabric (Zweigart 1235) in
    Ivory (colour 264) approximately 32 cm x
    15 cm (12½ in x 6 in)
DMC stranded cotton in colours indicated
    on the chart
Tapestry needle size 26
Small embroidery hoop
70 gm (2½ oz) polyester wadding, about 8
    cm x 32 cm (3 in x 12½ in)
Ivory brushed satin lining fabric, about 8
    cm x 32 cm (3 in x 12½ in)
50 cm (½ yd) pink satin bias binding
Dressmaking pins
Ivory and pink threads for machine
Tacking (basting) thread
Sewing needle
One sew-on press stud
*(See **Getting started** page 20 for making*
bias binding, joining bias binding and
binding raw edges)

Stitching the embroidery:
1 Place the rosebud centrally 5 cm (2 in) up from one of the short sides of the evenweave fabric.
2 Place the fabric in the hoop and follow the chart, stitching each cross over two threads in each direction.
3 Remove the work from the hoop and press lightly on the wrong side.

> **Note:** *If you prefer, you could substitute the ivory lining with a pastel colour to match the binding, or you could use a fine cotton with a delicate, floral mini print. You could then make bias binding from this fabric, and stitch narrow rouleau ties to use instead of ribbon.*

Making up the lipstick case:

1 Cut the embroidered fabric to make a narrow rectangle 5 cm x 29 cm (2 in x 12½ in), positioning the rosebud 2 cm (¾ in) from bottom edge. Withdraw threads as a guide for cutting and shaping the lower corners.
2 Cut a piece of lining and a piece of wadding to the same size.

3 Place the embroidered piece and the lining together with right sides facing and place the wadding behind. Stitch a 1.5 cm (⅝ in) seam across the top.

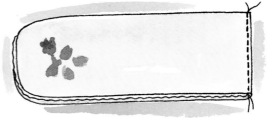

4 Trim the turnings, turn right sides out and press. Top-stitch close to the edge. Tack (baste) all the layers together.

5 Make a fold 9 cm (3½ in) from the top stitched edge to form a pocket. Tack (baste) it in place through all layers.

6 Pin and tack (baste) the bias binding all round the raw edges and across the bottom fold, placing the edge of the binding to the edge of the fabric and using the fold on the binding as the stitching line. Curve the lower corners to match the curve of the embroidered flap, and position the join so that it will be concealed at the back of the lipstick case.

7 Stitch the press stud to the underneath of the flap and the outer layer of the pocket.

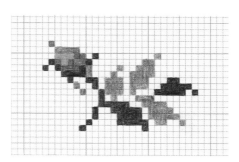

987 368 961 761 819 725 975

Trinket box

Glass-topped porcelain boxes make an ideal showcase for many small needlework projects. It is possible to make a pretty and personal gift in just a few hours; one that could quickly become something to be treasured, especially if it is made to commemorate a special occasion.

REQUIREMENTS
18 count Aida evenweave fabric (Zweigart 3793 colour 101 – Antique white) approximately 15 cm (6 in) square
DMC Flower thread – one skein of each colour as indicated on the chart
Tapestry needle size 26
Small embroidery hoop
Water-soluble pen
DMC oval trinket box N852 in blue

Stitching the embroidery:
1 Place the fabric in the embroidery hoop.
2 Following the chart and, using a single strand of thread, stitch the design working each cross over one block of threads.

Assembling the lid:
1 Remove the embroidery from the hoop and press lightly on the wrong side with the work face down on a clean soft towel.
2 Position the frame of the lid over the design so that the pansies are in the centre.

Draw round the lid lightly with the water-soluble pen.
3 Cut out the oval shape just inside the drawn line.
4 Assemble the lid according to the box maker's instructions.

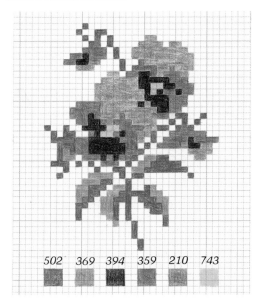

502 369 394 359 210 743

Pansies are said to represent thoughts, so they are the perfect flowers to decorate a trinket box which is designed for someone special.

Assisi-work paperweight

Assisi work is a form of counted-thread embroidery which originated in Italy in the 14th century.

The design is first outlined in Holbein stitch using a dark thread; the background is then filled-in with cross stitch of a single colour, traditionally red or blue.

REQUIREMENTS
Linda evenweave fabric (Zweigart 1235 colour 101 – Antique white) approximately 15 x 15 cm (6 x 6 in) square
DMC stranded cottons – one skein black and one blue number 798.
Tapestry needle size 26
Small embroidery hoop
Water-soluble pen
Small piece soft iron-on interfacing, approximately 9 x 9 cm (3½ x 3½ in) square
DMC round paperweight number N857
*(See **Getting started** page 17 for Holbein stitch)*

Stitching the embroidery:

1 Place the fabric in the embroidery hoop.
2 Using a single strand of black thread, follow the chart to work the outline of the design in Holbein stitch. Work each stitch over two threads of the fabric.
3 Using two strands of blue thread, fill in the background shapes as shown on the chart. Work each cross over two vertical and two horizontal threads of the fabric.

Assembling the paperweight:

1 Remove the embroidery from the hoop and press lightly on the wrong side, with the work face down on a clean soft towel.
2 Iron the interfacing on to the wrong side of the embroidery. (This will stop the fabric from fraying when the shape is cut out.)
3 Place the card disc supplied with the paperweight centrally over the embroidery, and draw round it lightly with the water-soluble pen.
4 Cut out just inside the line and remove any remaining pen marks with the corner of a damp cloth.
5 Place the embroidery face down in the back of the paperweight. Cover with the self-adhesive felt disc, following the paperweight maker's instructions.

Assisi work, with its clearly defined lines and strong colouring, has great appeal. This glass paper weight is a traditional desk-top gift, and would be a good choice for a man or woman. Blue is chosen for the stitching here, but you could substitute the other well-known Assisi-work colour red, or use green, ochre, or another colour to suit a particular colour scheme.

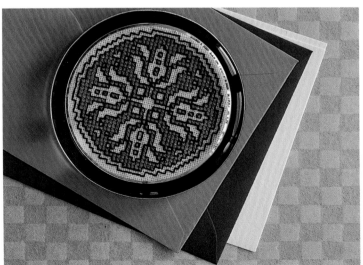

Scented sachets

Perfumed sachets have been popular for many centuries. Used to give a pleasant fragrance to clothes and linen, they also have the added advantage of helping to keep moths away. Many sweet smelling herbs and flowers can be used and the choice of filling is a personal one.

As a child, we had an annual ritual in which I was able to take part from an early age. Every summer we picked the lavender in the garden and laid it in the sun to dry. As Christmas came close, my mother would sew dozens of little bags which we would fill with the lavender as gifts. Today, a perfumed sachet is as welcome a gift as ever and easy to make, since lavender and pot pourris are readily available.

Both the pretty cat sachets here are made in the same way.

Lavender cat

REQUIREMENTS

14 count Aida evenweave fabric (Zweigart 3706 colour number 713) approximately 25 x 25 m (10 x 10 in) square

Lavender coloured satin approximately 20 cm x 18 cm (8 in x 7 in)
Matching sewing machine thread
3–4 tablespoons dried lavender

Pot pourri cat

REQUIREMENTS

14 count Aida evenweave fabric (Zweigart 3706 colour number 302) approximately 25 x 25 m (10 x 10 in) square
Pink satin, piece approximately 20 cm x 18 cm (8 in x 7 in)
Matching sewing machine thread
2–3 tablespoons pot pourri
For both sachets *you will need*
DMC stranded cottons – one skein of each colour as indicated on the charts
Tapestry needle size 26
Small embroidery hoop
Tracing paper
Pencil
Dress maker's carbon paper
Dressmaker's pins
Sewing needle
Tacking thread
Sticky tape

| 552 | 327 | 609 | 562 | 840 | B |

*(See **Getting started** page 17 for back stitch and French knots, page 21 for clipping curves, page 19 for slip stitch, and page 18 for using dressmaker's carbon paper)*

Stitching the embroidery:

1 Place the evenweave fabric in the embroidery hoop.

2 Work the cross stitch following the chart, and using two strands of thread. Work each cross over one block of threads.

3 Again, following the chart but using a single thread, work the back stitch around the eyes, nose and mouth.

4 Using two strands of brown thread, work a few French knots on each cheek for the cats' whiskers.

5 Remove the work from the hoop and press lightly on the wrong side with the embroidery face down on a clean soft towel.

These sweet little sachets will be favourites with all cat lovers. As an alternative filling, you could use padding and essential oils.

Making up the sachets:

1 Trace the outline of the cat on to tracing paper. Turn the tracing over and place it in position over the wrong side of the embroidery and secure with sticky tape.

2 Slip the carbon paper under the tracing and carefully draw over the lines, to transfer the cat shape on to the fabric. Remove the carbon and tracing.

3 Place the embroidery face down on the right side of the satin. Pin, tack (baste) and machine stitch along the transfer line, leaving a 6 cm (2⅜ in) opening along the bottom edge.

4 Remove tacking (basting) thread, and trim away the excess fabric to 6 mm (¼ in). Clip the curves.

5 Turn right sides out and press lightly under a clean cloth.

6 Using a small spoon, fill the sachet with lavender or pot pourri, taking care not to over-fill as this will make it harder to stitch the opening neatly.

7 Slip stitch the opening closed with small, neat stitches.

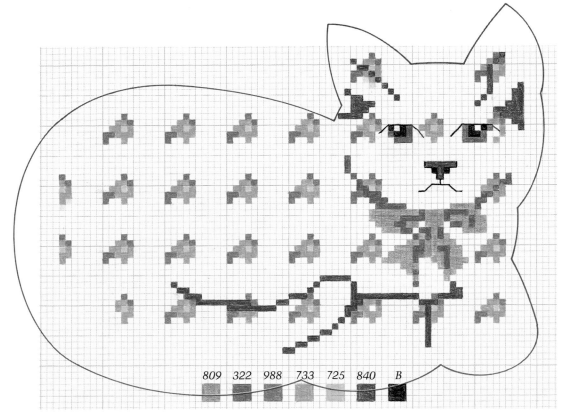

809	322	988	733	725	840	B

Spectacle case

Cross stitch worked in wool on canvas provides a firm thick fabric, and any spectacle wearer would be glad to receive an attractive case worked in this way to protect their lenses. This design would make an equally acceptable gift for either sex.

REQUIREMENTS
12 mesh White interlock canvas (Zweigart E604B) approximately 18 cm x 26 cm (18 in x 10 in)
DMC Medici wools: one skein of each colour indicated on the chart
Tapestry needle size 20
Straight sided frame if desired
Dark green velvet approximately 15 cm x 65 cm (6 in x 26 in)
Soft iron-on interfacing approximately 18 cm x 10 cm (7 in x 4 in)
Tacking (basting) thread
Sewing machine thread to match the velvet
Ordinary sewing needle
*(See **Getting started** page 15 for how to attach canvas to a frame if you prefer to work with one. (Cross stitch does not distort canvas, so this is not essential.) See also, page 13 for tips on working with*

Medici wools. See page 21 for clipping corners and page 19 for working hem stitch)

Stitching the embroidery:
1 Follow the chart, using two strands of wool and taking care not to pull the stitches too tight. Stitch each cross over one intersection of the canvas threads.
2 When the embroidery is completed, remove from the frame (if used), and place the work face down on a clean soft towel. Press lightly on the wrong side.

Making up the spectacle case:
1 Trim the canvas leaving 1 cm (3/8 in) all round the embroidery.
2 Cut a piece of velvet the same size as the canvas embroidery.
3 Iron a piece of interfacing to the wrong side of the velvet and trim away any excess.
4 Place the canvas and the velvet together with right sides facing. Pin, tack (baste) and machine stitch the layers together on the edge of the embroidery, leaving the top edge open. Remove the tacking (basting) thread.
5 Trim the turnings to 6 mm (1/4 in), but not at the top edge. Clip the corners and turn right side out to make a pocket. Press.

Making the lining:

1 Cut a second piece of velvet 39 cm x 10 cm (15¼ in x 4 in).

2 Fold in half with the short sides together and right side inside. Pin, tack (baste) and machine a 1.3 cm (½ in) seam down each long side, leaving the top open. Remove the tacking (basting) thread and trim the turnings. Clip the corners and press lightly under a clean cloth.

3 Insert the lining into the spectacle case so that the wrong sides are together and the side seams are matching. Leave 1.5 cm (⅝ in) protruding at the top.

4 Fold a double hem in the lining, making the first fold 6 mm (¼ in) and the second fold 1 cm (⅜ in) and pin to the outside of the spectacle case so that the edge of the hem meets the top of the embroidery.

5 Hem stitch in place with small stitches.

8505	8208	8027
8105	8408	8725

This cross stitch design on canvas is worked in wool, so it is both attractive and hardwearing.

Further reading

The following books are a constant source of ideas and inspiration:

A Sampler of Alphabets. Sterling Publishing Co. 1987.

Edmonds, Mary Jaene. *Samplers and Samplermakers.* Charles Letts, 1991.

Fasset, Kaffe. *Glorious Inspiration.* Century, 1991.

Gostelow, Mary. *Embroidery.* Marshall Cavendish Editions, 1977.

Ohms, Margaret. *Ethnic Embroidery.* Batsford, 1989.

Revault, Jacques. *Designs and Patterns from North African Carpets and Textiles.* Dover Publications, 1973.

Treasures from the Embroiderers' Guild Collection. David and Charles, 1991.

Useful addresses

I have used DMC threads and fabrics throughout this book. For details of your nearest stockist, contact the DMC subsidiaries listed here. In Great Britain, Australia and New Zealand, DMC handle Zweigart products.

Great Britain

DMC Creative World
Pullman Road
Wigston
Leicestershire LE18 2DY
England
Tel: 0533 811040

Framecraft Miniatures Ltd
148–150 High Street
Aston
Birmingham B6 4US
Tel: 021 359 4442

'Pisces'
26 High Street
Ewell Village
Surrey KT17 1SJ

'Pisces' mail order
113 St Denys Road
St Denys
Southampton SO2 1FS

Australia and New Zealand

DMC Needlecraft Pty, Ltd
51-66 Carrington Road
Marrickville
NSW 2204
Australia
Postal Address:
P.O. Box 317
Earlswood
NSW 2206

Kirsten Yarns Pty Ltd
216 Canterbury Road
Canterbury
VIC 3126
Tel: (03) 836 4385

Heather's Fabric Market
96 Bloomfield Street
Cleveland
QLD 4163
Tel: (07) 286 4969

Emtex Handcrafts Pty Ltd
7 Bellows Street
Welshpool
WA 6106
Tel: (09) 356 2392

Shann Accessories
10 Lyons Terrace
Windsor
QLD 4030
Tel: (07) 857 7255

Campbells Toys & Crafts
DMC Centre
31–33 Picton Street
Howick
Tel: (09) 534 1148

In Stitches
Broadway Plaza Shopping Centre
Newmarket
Tel: (09) 524 7149

La Châtelaine
451 Mt Eden Road
Mt Eden
Tel: (09) 631 0497

The Embroiderer
132 Hinemoa Street
Birkenhead
Tel: (09) 419 0900

Threadneedle Street
579 Manakau Road
Epsom
Tel: (09) 630 3870

Village Needlecrafts
67A Victoria Road
Devonport
Tel: (09) 445 1205

Warnaar Trading Co. Ltd
376 Ferry Road
PO Box 19567
Christchurch

Index